Thank you!

First of all, I would like to express my deepest gratitude to all those who have chosen to purchase and read this book. It is you, passionate readers, who make our work as authors and publishers possible..

I would love to hear your emotions, experiences, and opinions about the book. Every 5-star review is a way to share your enthusiasm and appreciation.

In addition to helping other readers make an informed purchasing decision, reviews are essential in improving the visibility and credibility of our work on Amazon.

It would be wonderful if you could dedicate a few minutes of your time to leave a review on the Amazon website.

Thank you again for choosing this book and for the time you dedicate to leaving a review

Thank you

THE CURSE BROKEN
How God Delivered Me From Darkness

A true story of obsessions, exorcisms and miraculous redemption

By
Emanuele Maida

Copyright © 2025
LDN Editions
www.ldnonline.org

THE BROKEN CURSE: How God Delivered Me From Darkness
A true story of obsessions, exorcisms and miraculous redemption

Copyright © 2025 Vincenzo Petrarca

All rights reserved. No part of this book may be reproduced in any manner or transmitted in any form or by any means, electronic or mechanical, including photocopying, recording, or any information retrieval system without the written permission of the author.

Foreword

Dear reader,

This book you have in your hands is not a simple story, nor a theoretical treatise on faith, but a living, suffered and redeemed testimony. It is the journey of a man who has gone through the dark night of the soul, who has experienced evil in its most concrete and devastating form, but who has found in the power of God the way to liberation and healing.

My name is Vincenzo Petrarca and my ministry, as an Apostle of the Evangelical Church, has led me over the years to clash with the deepest realities of the spiritual world, including the field of exorcism. I know that for many this theme may seem distant or even belonging to mythology or superstition. Yet, my experience, as well as that of many tormented souls I have accompanied, proves that evil is real, tangible, subtle and destructive.

The story you will read is that of Emanuele, an ordinary man who found himself fighting an invisible but very powerful evil. It is the story of those who have experienced despair, fear, spiritual oppression, but also grace, mercy and salvation in Christ. His walk is a hymn to hope and a concrete demonstration of what the Lord can do when we abandon ourselves completely to Him.

THE SPIRITUAL WORLD: A REALITY THAT CANNOT BE IGNORED

We live in a time when the supernatural is reduced to mere imagination or interpreted with psychological categories. However, Scripture clearly warns us: there is an invisible world, a kingdom of darkness that opposes God and that incessantly seeks to distance us from the truth. Satan is not a metaphor, but a real being, an adversary who lies behind many of the personal crises, inexplicable suffering, and oppression that befall man.

The biggest mistake we can make is to think that the devil does not exist. His cunning lies precisely in making us believe that it is just an invention. Yet, the scriptures remind us that the battle between good and evil is real: *"For our wrestling is not against flesh and blood, but against principalities, against powers, against the rulers of this world of darkness, against the spiritual forces of wickedness in the heavenly places" (Ephesians 6:12).*

THE POWER OF FAITH AND THE VICTORY OF CHRIST

The good news is that the final victory has already been won by Jesus Christ on the cross. His sacrifice broke the chains of death and sin, defeated the powers of darkness, and opened the way to salvation for all who believe in Him.

"I have given you power to walk upon serpents and scorpions and upon all the power of the enemy; nothing can harm you" (Luke 10:19).

This promise is not just for a select few, but for every child of God who chooses to trust Him. Through prayer, the sacraments, the Word, and a life of obedience to God, every Christian can resist the attacks of the evil one and live a life of freedom and fullness in Christ.

AN INVITATION TO REFLECTION AND CONVERSION

This book is not only the story of Emanuele, but it could be the story of many. It could be your story. In these pages you will find profound questions, moments of crisis and, above all, the reflection of a God who never abandons His children. If you are going through a difficult period, if you feel that something in your life is weighing you down and dragging you into darkness, know that there is hope. The path to liberation exists and passes through a clear decision: to choose Christ, to entrust one's life to him and to allow him to act.

Every page of this book is an invitation to open our eyes, to recognize the enemy, but above all to trust in the power of the Lord. No matter how deep the wounds, no matter how dark the night, *"the light shines in the darkness, and the darkness has not overpowered it" (John 1:5).*

I invite you, therefore, to read these pages with an open heart, letting the Holy Spirit speak to you. May this testimony be an encouragement to you, may it awaken in you the desire for a new life, free and full of God's grace.

May the Lord bless you and guide you on the path of truth and freedom.

Enjoy the reading

Apostle Vincent Petrarch

Introduction

There are experiences in life that mark us forever. There are events that leave an indelible imprint on the heart, that change the way we see the world and understand reality. This book was born from one of these experiences, from a story lived on my skin, suffered in the depths of my soul, but also redeemed by God's grace.

A SPECIAL DEDICATION

I want to dedicate these pages to a dear friend who is no longer with me today, who left this world because of an illness. His absence is a void that no words can ever fill, but his memory is a constant presence in my heart.

"Even though you are no longer physically here, your spirit will continue to live in me. Every memory you left me is a piece of you that I will always carry in my heart."

Life is a breath, yet in that brief moment that is granted to us on this earth, we can leave an indelible mark. My friend did it with his goodness, with his strength, with his ability to face suffering with dignity and hope. **This book is also for him.**

THE STRUGGLE BETWEEN GOOD AND EVIL: AN EVER-PRESENT REALITY

Since the beginning of time, humanity has witnessed and experienced the conflict between good and evil. An invisible battle that is not only fought in biblical stories, but that is still alive today, more real than one can imagine.

Every day, in our choices, in our thoughts, in our gestures, this struggle manifests itself. There is a force that pushes towards light, towards truth, towards love. And there is another that tries to drag us into the shadows, that wants to annihilate our identity and our hope.

Agency is the greatest gift God has given us, but it is also our greatest responsibility. We are called to choose every day: **to follow the light or**

to let ourselves be swallowed up by the darkness?

Already in the Old Testament we find the first example of this choice: **Adam and Eve in the Garden of Eden.** God had given them everything, the freedom to live in harmony with Him, but also the free will to choose. **And they chose to disobey.**

That choice had consequences for all of humanity. Today we are no longer in a perfect garden, but in a world where sin, suffering and evil seem to have the upper hand. Yet, **God has always left open a way back**.

"If you are overwhelmed by the world with all its snares, dangerous deceptions, you must firmly believe that God has conquered death, the world, and put your life in his hands. In His name there is power, victory, deliverance."

When we go through moments of darkness, when we feel overwhelmed by pain and fear, we must ask ourselves a fundamental question:

"Lord, why do you allow this? What exactly do I need to understand?"

The answer is not always immediate, but it is the first step towards salvation.

WHY I DECIDED TO WRITE THIS BOOK

This story is not just my story. It is the story of anyone who has experienced suffering, of anyone who has found themselves fighting against something greater than themselves, of anyone who has felt the weight of darkness on their soul and has sought a way out.

My life has been overwhelmed by events that I never imagined. I have known evil in a form that I did not believe possible, I have been overwhelmed by a reality that was beyond my comprehension, I have touched the deepest pain with my own hands. **But in that darkness, I encountered the light of God.**

I am not writing this book to scare or to tell an extraordinary story. **I write this because I know that there are people who are going through the same journey and do not know where to look for help.**

"Since I was converted, I have seen the hand of God upon me. He followed me, he guided me, he got me up when I fell. Today I know that my walk has a purpose: to help others find the way to deliverance and peace in Christ."

God never abandons us, even when it seems that all is lost.

THE DESCENT INTO DARKNESS AND THE SEARCH FOR LIGHT

I had always heard of evil. **But it is one thing to hear about it, another to experience it on your own skin.**

I knew that the devil exists, that evil is an active force in the world. But I never thought he could hit me in such a direct, devastating, violent way.

It was not by my choice that I entered this battle. I entered it due to circumstances beyond my control. **I was the victim of a dark action that turned my existence upside down.**

Suddenly, everything I thought I knew about myself was questioned. My balance has been destroyed, my peace annihilated. **Evil tried to take control of my life.**

Yet, **God has never stopped looking for me**.

"Emanuele faces all this with courage. Something is broken, and he embarks on a path of true conversion, on a psychological and religious basis, which will help him to discover who God really is, the only one who can heal the deepest wounds, until he regains possession of his true identity in Christ."

A STORY OF FALLS AND REBIRTHS

It has not been an easy path. There were moments of discouragement, anger, despair. I was afraid, I doubted, I fought against myself and against what was happening to me.

But God has never stopped reaching out to me.

"At some point in life, your existence changes suddenly. Suffocating mists surround you, they want to swallow you. You have only one choice: let yourself be swallowed up or react with a true U-turn."

I chose to react. I chose to fight for my soul. I have chosen to believe that **God is greater than evil, that His grace is stronger than any darkness**.

AN INVITATION TO READ

I have not yet reached the end of the journey. **None of us are.** We are all on a journey, day after day, learning to trust God, letting ourselves be transformed by His grace.

If you are reading these pages, perhaps you too are looking for answers.

I invite you to read this book **without prejudice, with an open heart**. Ask the Holy Ghost to guide you, to show you what needs to be healed within you.

If my experience can help even one person find the way to salvation, then all of this will have made sense.

To God be the glory.

Emanuele Maida

CHAPTER 1
Who are you sir?

Life often asks us questions that we are not prepared to answer. We grow up with certainties, with an idea of who we are and what our place in the world is. But then, one day, something happens. An event, a meeting, a moment of crisis, and everything we thought we knew crumbles like sand between our fingers. We suddenly find ourselves disoriented, our hearts swollen with questions: **Who am I really? What is the meaning of my life? And above all, who is God? Do I really know Him, or do I just have an idea of Him built on what I was taught?**

THE ORIGINS: A FAITH HANDED DOWN, BUT NOT LIVED

I was born and raised in a Catholic family, one of those in which faith is part of everyday life, but more as a habit than as a living experience. God was present in my childhood, but he was a distant God, almost an idea rather than a person. People prayed before eating, went to Mass on Sundays, and did the sacraments according to the calendar established by tradition.

But can I say that **I really knew him?**

No.

Mine was a faith learned, but not internalized. God was for me a concept, a distant entity, a severe judge rather than a loving Father. I imagined Him as someone who watched from above, ready to punish my mistakes, but I rarely thought of Him as someone with whom I could have a genuine relationship.

And so, growing up, I found myself living a façade religiosity, made up of external practices, but devoid of a true inner experience.

LONELINESS AND THE DESIRE TO BELONG

I was a reserved, shy boy, often closed in my thoughts. I felt a strong need to belong, to find my place in the world, but I struggled to relate to others. My shyness made me insecure, unable to fully express what I felt.

In an effort to find a community, I approached **Communion and Liberation**, a widespread Catholic movement. At first it seemed like the right place for me. We talked about God, lived the faith in groups, shared experiences of prayer and formation. Yet, despite the years spent in that context, I felt that I didn't really belong.

I was in a religious movement, but my soul was still far from God.

I couldn't make deep bonds, I always felt one step behind the others. I saw them so confident, so convinced, while I continued to carry within me a sense of emptiness that I could not fill.

After a long time, I made a decision: **to leave the movement**.

I didn't really know what I was looking for, but one thing was certain: **I had to find him elsewhere**.

THE CHANGE OF LIFE AND THE ILLUSION OF HAVING FOUND A WAY

Over the years, my family decided to move to another district of Turin, in the Madonna di Campagna area. Here, in a new environment, I had the opportunity to start over.

Attending the neighborhood oratory, I finally began to feel part of something. I became an **assistant catechist** for the children, an experience that gave me moments of joy and satisfaction. There was something pure about being with them, about telling stories about Jesus, about seeing their eyes shine with curiosity and simple faith.

At that time I also started going out with a group of friends, boys and girls between twenty-five and thirty years old. We shared moments of leisure, we went to the cinema, we organized outings. **And for the first time I felt less alone.**

But, despite everything, my heart was still restless.

I had found companionship, but I had not yet found God.

I was happy at times, but inside I knew that something was missing.

THE ENCOUNTER WITH RENEWAL IN THE SPIRIT

It was at this time that, through a friend, I learned about a prayer group called **Renewal in the Spirit**.

I didn't really know what to expect. I just knew that it was a different experience from the one I had lived up to that moment. And so, almost out of curiosity, I accepted the invitation and attended one of their meetings.

What I saw left me displaced.

It was not a simple prayer meeting. It was something alive, engaging. We praised God with songs, prayed fervently, read the Word with an intensity that I had never experienced before. **There was a palpable joy, an energy that I could not explain, a presence that could be felt in the air.**

For the first time in my life, I asked myself:

"What if God was really here? What if it was something more than a concept? What if he were a living and real person, eager to enter into a relationship with me?"

I still didn't know how to answer these questions, but I felt that I had to keep looking.

And so, week after week, I went back to the meetings.

THE QUESTION THAT CHANGES EVERYTHING

It was in that context that I began to ask myself the question that would change everything:

"Lord, have I ever really known you?"

I realized that, up to that point, my faith had been built on notions, rituals, habits. But not about a personal encounter with God.

The Bible tells of a man, a Pharisee named Nicodemus, who came to Jesus at night to seek answers. He was an educated man, a master of the law, yet he knew he was missing something.

Jesus said to him:

"Truly, truly, I say unto thee, unless one is born again, he cannot see the kingdom of God" (John 3:3).

Those words began to resonate within me.

Maybe I needed **to be born again**, too.

It was not enough to have grown up in a Catholic family. It was not enough to have attended prayer groups. It was not enough to know the prayers by heart. **I had to meet God personally.**

And so, not yet knowing where this path would lead me, **I began to really look for it**.

Little did I know that this search would lead me down a path of trials, battles, and shocking revelations.

I didn't know that my journey would pass through darkness before arriving at the light.

But one thing was certain: **my life would never be the same again.**

CHAPTER 2

The meeting that changed everything

2014 was a year I would never forget. I was 32 years old and, like many other times, I found myself reflecting on my life, on the changes I had faced, on the roads I had traveled up to that moment. I thought I had achieved a certain balance, albeit fragile, between my faith and my daily life. I couldn't imagine that everything would change shortly thereafter.

One evening like many others, a friend suggested that I go out. It was one of those evenings when you don't expect anything special: just two friends who decide to have fun, to break the monotony of the routine. But that evening proved decisive.

While we were chatting, my friend confided in me that there was a girl who had expressed interest in me. He said that he had seen me in the area, that we knew each other by sight. She explained to me that sometimes they went out together, that she found her nice, interesting, and that maybe it would be nice if I knew her too.

I didn't usually take acquaintances lightly, and yet, that evening, something pushed me to accept. **Maybe it was the need for company, maybe curiosity. Or maybe there was already a bigger design in place, a design that I still didn't understand.**

The girl's name was **Alessandra**.

THE FIRST IMPRESSION: A WELL-CONSTRUCTED MASK

When I met her, Alessandra immediately seemed to me a pleasant person. She was smiling, spoke confidently, seemed like a sweet girl, and most importantly, shared my faith. He told me that he attended the **Renewal in the Spirit**, just like me. This information reassured me: if he was part of a journey of faith, then he could only be a respectable, reliable person.

We started dating lightly, without any particular expectations. Our outings were simple: a walk, a chat, a few evenings with friends. There was nothing strange about her, at least apparently. Yet, something in me was not completely convinced.

As the months passed, I felt that there was **a veil of ambiguity** in his behavior. There were details that didn't fit together, phrases that puzzled me, looks that seemed to escape when I tried to grasp the truth in his eyes.

THE MASK THAT FALLS

It wasn't until after a couple of months that I began to notice details that I could no longer ignore.

Alexandra, despite her apparent participation in the Renewal in the Spirit, **did not live the faith authentically**. It was as if he was only physically present, as if the words he said had no weight in his heart.

The Word of God says:

"For the children of this world are more shrewd than the children of the Light toward their equals" (Luke 16:8).

The more I got to know her, the more I felt a feeling of unease inside me.

One day, while we were together, I noticed something disturbing: there were **deep cuts** on his arms, marks that seemed to have been made intentionally.

I froze. **Why did a girl who said she had faith, who said she prayed, have those marks on her body?**

I tried to talk to her, to ask her what had happened, but she minimized, changed the subject.

He told me about his family: an **alcoholic** father, a **Buddhist** mother, a family environment that seemed to be a mixture of pain and spiritual confusion.

Every detail that emerged gave me an increasingly strong certainty in my heart: **I had to interrupt this acquaintance.**

Not out of judgment, not out of fear, but because I felt a clear warning within me: **this relationship did not come from God.**

It was as if an inner voice was telling me to leave before it was too late.

THE DECISION TO CLOSE AND THE BEGINNING OF THE DRAMA

One evening, I decided to break up with Alessandra.

I wanted to be clear, direct, but without hurting her. I proposed that we meet one last time, to talk calmly, to explain my decision.

That evening we went to eat a pizza and then an ice cream.

It seemed like a quiet evening, one of those in which a chapter closes with serenity. But in reality **that** was the evening that marked the beginning of my nightmare.

That was **the evening of the "short circuit".**

THE SHORT CIRCUIT: EVIL MANIFESTS ITSELF

After that last evening with Alessandra, **my life changed drastically**.

At first it was just a sense of unease, a strange anxiety that I couldn't explain.

Then, within a few days, my mind and body began to be overwhelmed by something dark.

I experienced **violent bouts of depression**, paralyzing anxiety attacks, insomnia, intrusive and destructive thoughts.

I was afraid of everything: of people, of everyday situations, even of my own shadow. **I felt followed, observed.**

At night, my room became a place of torment. **Terrible nightmares**, visions of monsters, inexplicable noises. I woke up with a start, drenched in sweat, with my heart beating wildly.

A strange aversion to the sacred **began to manifest itself**.

Every time I entered the church, I felt an unbearable weight on my chest, my strength left me, my mind filled with horrible thoughts. **I could no longer pray, I could no longer bear the presence of the Eucharist.**

THE SEARCH FOR AN ANSWER: MEDICINE OR SPIRITUALITY?

My condition was getting worse day by day.

I decided to go to a doctor. The neurologist diagnosed me **with severe depression with nervous breakdown** and prescribed **antidepressants**.

Yet, deep down, **I knew that the problem was not just psychological**.

The medicines helped me sleep, but they didn't give me peace. **I felt that my soul was sick, more than my body.**

It was then that I understood a great truth: **there are wounds that medicine cannot heal, pains that belong not only to the mind, but also to the spirit.**

I had entered a battle that I could not fight alone.

I needed God.

TOWARDS AN ANSWER

This experience opened my eyes to a reality that until then I had never seriously considered: **spiritual evil exists, and it is more real than we think.**

That period was one of the hardest of my life, but it was also the beginning of a path that would lead me to a new awareness.

I wasn't just sick. **I was under attack.**

And to get out of it, human care was not enough. **God's power was needed.**

That awareness pushed me to look for answers.

And it was then that my real journey began.

Chapter 3
God heals wounds and our masks

I have always loved the story of the resurrection of Lazarus. There is something extraordinary in that Gospel episode, something that speaks directly to the soul of every man and woman. Lazarus was not simply dead, he **had already been buried for four days**. His body was in a state of decomposition, his tomb gave off **an unbearable smell**.

When Jesus arrived, Martha warned him:

"Lord, already send forth a bad smell, for it is four days old" (John 11:39).

This phrase has always struck me. How many times in our lives have we been afraid to show God our deepest pain? How many times have we preferred **to keep the tomb of our wounds closed**, convinced that no one can bear the stench?

Yet, Jesus is not afraid of our pain. **He does not shrink from our misery, he does not feel disgust for our weaknesses.** On the contrary, he draws near, bends over us, enters those dark places that we ourselves do not dare to look at.

When everything inside us screams:

"No, Lord! Do not open this tomb! There is only death and despair in here!"

He answers us with love:

"I can measure myself against your bad smell, because I am God. I won't leave you in there. I love you."

And it is at that moment that **life is reborn**, that hope is rekindled, that the chains of despair are broken.

But the real question is, **"Will you let Jesus heal you?"**

THE RISK OF BEING TRAPPED BY WOUNDS

The wounds of the soul are like deep cuts that do not want to heal. **Some are visible, others are hidden. Some come from painful life experiences, others are the result of spiritual battles that we don't even know we're fighting.**

If they are not healed, the wounds do not disappear. They turn into **ballast**, into burdens that prevent us from living fully. They make us distrustful, closed, full of fear.

The problem is that we often do not want to face them.

We cover them with masks.

The mask of strength: *"I'm fine, I don't need help."*
The mask of indifference: *"It's over now, I don't think about it anymore."*
The mask of rationality: *"It's just a psychological problem, I can solve it myself."*

But deep in our hearts we know that **we are just running away**.

And the more we try to ignore them, the more the wounds find a way to make themselves felt. **Through anxiety, depression, anger, mistrust, fear.**

Jesus, on the other hand, tells us:

"If you want, I can heal you. But you have to allow it."

GOD DOESN'T FOLLOW SHORTCUTS

God could heal our wounds in an instant, yet often He does not do it right away.

Because?

Because **God is not only interested in healing the symptoms, He wants to heal the root.**

If a wound is deep, it is not enough to cover it with a plaster. **It must be cleaned, it must be disinfected, it must be allowed to heal slowly, with the necessary time.**

And this process can hurt.

Sometimes God leads us **to relive our pain**, not because he wants to make us suffer, but because he knows that **only through it can we truly heal.**

Jesus did not come to give us a life without difficulties. He came to give us a **redeemed** life, transformed by His grace.

THE WOUNDS OF THE SOUL: SLITS OF DIVINE GRACE

In the world there is a lot of talk about **physical and mental well-being**, but spiritual well-being is neglected.

Yet, much suffering is not only psychological. **They are spiritual.**

A psychological wound can be healed with therapy, but a spiritual wound can only be healed by God.

"Suffering is useless," some say.

That's not true.

Suffering serves to make us cry out, to make us aware of our inner disorder.

If everything were always going well, **we would never feel the need for God.**

This is why, paradoxically, **our wounds can become the place where God meets us.**

If we let it.

THE MASKS I WORE

I myself, before recognizing my need for healing, **had hidden behind many masks.**

1. **The mask of injustice**
   "Why is all this happening to me?"

I felt like a victim of a cruel fate. I rebelled, I didn't understand. **My wound made me see the world in black and white.**

2. **The mask of loss of identity**
   "Who am I really? Am I Emanuele healthy or Emanuele sick?"

I was afraid I didn't know who I was anymore. My suffering had turned me into a person I no longer recognized.

But God has healed all this. **Day after day, He brought me back to my true identity in Him.**

CHAPTER 4
God, where are you?

There are times in life when we feel like we are losing everything. Moments in which the certainties we took for granted are shaken, in which what we thought safe vanishes into thin air. And so we ask ourselves: **God, where are you? Why do you allow all this?**

These are questions that arise from pain, suffering, fear. Yet, instead of rejecting them, we should learn to listen to them. Because behind these questions lies a deeper truth: **What is it in our hearts that makes us suffer so much? What are we clinging to so strongly that we feel that, without it, our lives lose meaning?**

If the pain becomes so great that we doubt God's mercy, **we need not fear**. We are not the first to feel this way. **Even the great men of the Bible have gone through the desert of doubt and trial.**

"My God, my God, why have you forsaken me?" (Psalm 22:1)

Jesus too, on the cross, spoke these words. **God knows that suffering is a difficult burden to bear.** But it does not leave us alone. Even when everything seems dark to us, **He is working.**

Our life, after all, is **a continuous preparation for the encounter with God**. Every trial, every suffering, every moment of difficulty is not there to destroy us, but to **purify us, to teach us to trust Him.**

It is not the number of years we live that enriches us. **What matters is the quality of life we live.**

Every day is **a gift from God to start again.**

THE PRUNING OF FAITH: THE PAIN THAT PREPARES THE FRUITS

Imagine a tree.

Every year, to make it grow stronger and healthier, the farmer must prune it. Cut off the dead branches, remove those that are too weak, let the sap focus only on the branches that will bear fruit.

If the tree had a voice, perhaps it would say, **"Why are you doing this to me? Why do you take away what is part of me?"**

Yet, pruning is **an act of love**.

"Every branch that bears fruit the Father prunes, that it may bear more fruit" (John 15:2).

Our faith is also pruned. **God allows pain to strengthen us, to make us grow, to make us more fruitful in the spiritual life.**

But when we find ourselves in that moment, when the blade of suffering touches us, we tend to rebel. **We want to understand why right away.**

Yet, the farmer does not explain to the tree why he is pruning it. **It just does it.**

God does the same with us. **He asks us to trust.**

THE DOUBT THAT TOOK ME AWAY FROM GOD

It is not easy to accept this truth. I myself, when I lived through the darkest period of my life, **turned away from prayer.**

I wondered, **"If God loves me, why does He allow so much pain? Why doesn't he free me?"**

My mind was full of questions, anger, anguish. **I was physically present at the prayer group, but my heart was far away.**

I felt alone. I felt abandoned.

Yet, God's Word reminds us:

"Don't worry about your life, what you're going to eat or wear. Look at the birds: they do not sow and they do not reap, yet the heavenly Father feeds them. Aren't you worth much more than them?" (Luke 12:25)

My suffering seemed **like an insurmountable mountain** to me.

How do almost all of us react to trials?

We sit in front of the climb, we complain, we convince ourselves that it is too big to face. **Yet God tells us, "I am with you. I will give you strength."**

Chapter 5

The knowledge of Paola and the new problems.

Love is one of the greatest desires of the human heart. It is that deep bond that makes us feel understood, accepted, valued. I too, in those years, looked for it with sincerity, hoping to find a partner with whom to share my faith and my life journey.

That's how I met **Paola**. Our meeting took place in an unusual way, through the internet. A medium that, I admit, aroused some distrust in me. I had never had experiences of this type and I had never trusted relationships born behind a screen. But at that moment in my life I was open to new possibilities.

Paola struck me right away. She was a sweet-looking girl, with a deep gaze and a way of speaking that conveyed sensitivity. Our knowledge quickly deepened. We discovered that we had many things in common: she also declared herself a believer, attended Church and had values apparently similar to mine.

Everything seemed perfect. I felt that God was finally giving me that stable and serene relationship I had desired. We spent a lot of time together, talking about dreams, projects, life. He introduced me to his family, I met his mother and grandparents. It seemed like an important step, a sign that she too saw a future together.

I remember with particular emotion the evening when he decided to participate in my prayer group. I was surprised and at the same time enthusiastic: it is not often that you meet someone who wants to actively share their faith. **It seemed to me the confirmation that everything was going in the right direction.**

But the reality often turns out to be different from how it appears at the beginning.

THE BEGINNING OF THE CRISIS

After months of relationship, something began to change. **His words and attitudes were no longer the same.** He did not understand my desire to live chastity until marriage and, over time, this divergence became a reason for continuous tension.

"But why do we have to deprive ourselves of something natural?" he often told me. "If we love each other, what's the point of waiting?"

At first I tried to explain my point of view to her calmly, with love, convinced that she understood the beauty of my choice. But time passed, and his insistence became heavier and heavier. **I felt pressured, judged, almost ridiculed for my desire to follow a path different from the one imposed by the world.**

It wasn't just a matter of different ideas, it was a real inner battle. I began to doubt: **what if I was the wrong one?** What if my way of living the faith was just an illusion, a self-imposed limit that was depriving me of happiness?

It was a difficult time. Every day I found myself fighting between fidelity to my values and the fear of losing that relationship I had wanted so much. I was trying to heal from past wounds, and instead I felt like I was entering a new vortex of pain.

THE FIRST SIGNS OF A DECEPTION

To make matters worse, another detail began to trouble me deeply. One day, talking about her past and her family, Paola told me some episodes related to her grandmother.

"My grandmother has special powers," she said naturally. **"She has always been able to heal people with the energy of her hands."**

His words set off alarm bells in me. **What exactly did he mean?** I asked her to explain better and she told me that her grandmother practiced **pranotherapy**, a healing method based on an alleged flow of energy that would flow in the human body through the so-called "chakras".

Not only that: **he also frequented a magician** to get advice and "protection".

I felt my blood run cold. Once again, as had already happened with Alessandra, I found myself in contact with something dark, spiritually dangerous.

At first, I tried not to jump to conclusions. I decided to deepen the subject, to document myself. **The truth I discovered shocked me.**

THE DECEPTION OF PRANOTHERAPY

Many today speak of "energies", of "alternative healing", of "power of the hands". But behind these practices lies something much deeper and more deceptive.

Pranotherapy has its roots in **Indian Tantrism**, a practice that has nothing to do with the Christian faith. It is based on the idea that there are seven energy centers in the human body – the chakras – and that by manipulating these flows you can affect physical and mental health.

But God's Word warns us against all this:

"Take care that no one deceives you with his philosophy and empty deceptions inspired by human tradition, according to the elements of the world and not according to Christ." *(Colossians 2:8)*

The Church itself warns against these practices, which **do not come from God** and often open doors to negative spiritual influences.

After delving into the subject, I realized that I could not ignore what was happening. **Paola and her family believed in something that went against my faith.** I couldn't close my eyes.

THE END OF THE RELATIONSHIP

Despite the pain, I made the most difficult decision: **I left Paola**.

It was a painful separation, because part of me wanted to believe that it could change, that we could overcome those differences. But I knew that I could not compromise my faith, my integrity, just for fear of being alone.

God had already freed me once from a wrong bond. Now he was doing the same, even if I didn't fully understand it at the time.

Paola did not accept my decision well. He treated me coldly, with malice. **He cheated on me with another man, perhaps out of spite, perhaps out of anger.** I found out only months later, and it was another blow to the heart.

For a long time I felt lost. **God, why more suffering?**

But the truth is, **God wasn't punishing me.** He was protecting me, he was guiding me off a dangerous path, even though I still couldn't see him.

ANOTHER LESSON OF FAITH

I removed prayer from my life. I could no longer understand God's plan. **Why every time I tried to build something, everything seemed to collapse?**

It was only after years that I realized that **every wound, every disappointment, every loss, was actually a door that God closed to save me from something worse.**

The ways of the Lord are mysterious, but always right.

I was hurt, but I wasn't defeated. Even though I didn't know it yet, **God was preparing something much bigger for me.**

CHAPTER 6
The return to faith and rebirth

After so many wounds, so many disappointed hopes and so many interrupted paths, I found myself once again **far from God**. I had left my Renewal in the *Spirit group* and I felt a deep emptiness inside me. It was not only loneliness that weighed heavily, but the feeling of having lost myself, of having deviated from the path that God had traced for me.

It was at that time that I met **Alice**.

It was May, the Marian month, and in my apartment building we recited rosaries, as per tradition. I participated almost out of habit, without a real spiritual impulse. **I never imagined that right there, at that moment, God was about to put me back on the right path.**

Among the people present, I noticed **Alice**. He had a serene face, a collected attitude, a look that expressed a peace that I, at that moment, could no longer find.

God had put a new person in my path, but I still didn't understand why.

A short time later, I discovered a detail that struck me deeply: **Alice was attending a group of the Renewal in the Holy Spirit**. It was not a coincidence. Nothing is in God's plan.

I felt the desire to contact her, but I didn't know how. We had no friends in common, nor other opportunities to meet. So I took courage and wrote to her on Facebook. **A simple gesture, but one that would have changed my life.**

I told her that I was in a complicated moment in my faith and that, if it were God's will, I hoped to find a new prayer group to start over.

Time passed. No answer.

I thought my message had been lost, forgotten. **But God's times are not our times.**

After a year, Alice answered.

It was a surprise, but also a confirmation: God was working, silently, preparing the right moment for me to return to Him.

THE NEW PRAYER GROUP AND THE BEGINNING OF A STORY

I accepted his invitation and went to his prayer group. I remember that first evening well: **a mixture of emotion and fear.** What if I had not been accepted? What if it wasn't the right place for me?

But God had already prepared everything. I immediately felt at home.

Little by little I began to attend the group regularly, **returning to prayer, to fraternal communion, to the living presence of the Holy Spirit.**

And in the meantime, Alice and I began to get to know each other better.

At the beginning it was just a friendship, a bond built in the context of the group. But over time our relationship deepened, until it became something more.

We became a couple on a special day: the day in Turin they opened the Cathedral to allow the faithful to visit the Holy Shroud.

A sign of grace.

It seemed incredible to me: after so much suffering, God was finally giving me a solid love, founded on faith, blessed by heaven.

THE DREAM OF MARRIAGE AND THE UNEXPECTED TURNING POINT

Two and a half years **passed**. Alice and I were happy, we built our relationship day after day with commitment and dedication.

And so came **the big decision**: to get married.

We were convinced that it was God's will for us. We began the preparations: the house, the parties with the families, the details of the ceremony. **Everything was ready.**

But just when everything seemed to be defined, **something inside me changed**.

I felt a deep restlessness, an inner voice telling me to **stop**.

It was not fear, nor human indecision. **It was as if God Himself was asking me not to go on.**

It seemed absurd to me. **Why now? Why interrupt everything when we were so close to marriage?**

Yet, the more I tried to ignore that feeling, the stronger it became.

In the end, I made a drastic decision: to **annul the marriage.**

THE QUARREL AND THE SEPARATION

When I talked about it with Alice, the reaction was predictable: **a very hard fight**.

The words were heavy, the emotions violent. **It was too much pain for both of them to bear.**

We parted suddenly, abruptly. **It was a goodbye full of suffering.**

For a long time we did not see or hear from each other anymore.

I tried to go on alone. But **I felt like I was in a never-ending vicious circle**. Every time I thought I had found stability, something collapsed.

Once again I asked myself, **"God, why?"**

But the answer came much later.

Only in time did I realize that **this marriage was not in God's plan for my life.**

Alice had been a gift, but she wasn't the person God wanted me to share my life with.

THE SUPPORT OF A PRIEST AND SPIRITUAL REBIRTH

It was at that time that I decided to have **a priest follow me**.

He was not just any priest. **He was a man of great discernment, with a deep knowledge of human spirituality and psychology.**

I told him everything: **my wounds, my fears, my inner struggles.**

And he listened to me.

Never had anyone understood me so deeply.

It was he who made me reflect on a fundamental point: **the problems I was experiencing were not only emotional or psychological, but also spiritual.**

He said to me:

"First heal and then God will speak to you. Health first, then your future."

Those words struck me.

For the first time, I began to look at my path from a different perspective. **What if God was using all that pain to show me a new way?**

THE BEGINNING OF TRUE CONVERSION

It was that priest who gave me another precious piece of advice:

"Live the cross that God is allowing you, you will understand where it will take you. But don't run away. Live it."

All my life I had tried **to escape suffering**, to avoid it, to fight it.

Now I understood that **the cross was not an enemy, but an instrument of salvation.**

From that moment on, my life changed.

I accepted my story, my wounds, my disappointments.

I understood that **God had not abandoned me**, but was lovingly guiding me towards a destiny that I could not yet see.

That period marked **the beginning of my true conversion.**

From that moment, I would never be the same.

God had begun to mold something new in me.

And the journey had just begun.

CHAPTER 7
Living the Cross: A Path of Transformation

The Christian life is not a point of arrival, but a **continuous journey of conversion**. Every day we are called to grow, to renew ourselves, to get up after falls. **We never get to the top until we meet God face to face.**

Yet, along the way, we are often faced with **painful trials**, crosses that seem unbearable to us. Illness, loss, betrayal, loneliness... Each of us carries his own weight on his shoulders.

And then the question arises: **why?**

Why does God allow all this? Why does the journey of faith, which should be a path of peace, often pass through pain?

The answer is hidden in the mystery of the Cross.

Jesus himself, despite being the Son of God, went through the greatest suffering. He did not seek it, he did not desire it, but **when it arrived, he embraced it with love, transforming it into salvation.**

And we are called to do the same.

THE PAIN THAT DESTROYS AND THE PAIN THAT BUILDS

There are two types of suffering:

- **The one that destroys us**, caused by the envy, deception, arrogance and malice of others. This suffering must be avoided, because it is born of sin and brings only inner death.

- **The one that builds us**, that God allows to purify us, to make us stronger, more true, more similar to Him.

God does not want our pain, but uses it for our good.

It is written in the book of the prophet Jeremiah:

"I have plans for peace and not for misfortune. You will call on me, and I will hear you: I will gather you from all the nations where I have scattered you." (Jeremiah 29)

God is not a cruel judge who is pleased with our suffering. **God is a Father who loves us, even in pain.**

But how can one live the cross without being crushed by it?

THE POWER OF PRAYER AND THE WORD OF GOD

During the darkest period of my life, when the pain seemed to suffocate me, I did only one thing: **pray.**

Pray with all your heart.

Not a superficial prayer, made only with the lips, but a deep cry, a cry of the soul:

"Lord, if you are there, let me understand how to live this pain. Don't leave me alone. Help me not to flee, but to find You within this suffering."

And God answered.

Not with an audible voice, not with an instantaneous miracle, but **with His presence.**

He guided me to pick up the Bible and look for its promises.

One of the passages that spoke to me the most is **Psalm 33**:

"I bless the Lord at all times, on my lips always his praise. I question the Lord and He answers me, freeing me from all my anguish."

God's Word began to transform me from within.

Slowly I understood that **pain should not be a burden to be borne, but a springboard for my spiritual growth.**

GOD DOES NOT SEND THE CROSS, BUT TRANSFORMS IT INTO VICTORY

One of the biggest mistakes we can make in the Christian life is to think that **God sends us pain to test us**.

Many believe that suffering is a test, a kind of test to be passed to prove our faith.

But **this is not the case.**

God does not send the cross, he does not create evil, he does not rejoice in seeing us suffer.

The crosses of life come for three main reasons:

1. **The wrong choices of others** – Sin and selfishness of men bring pain to the world. Envy, betrayal, deception... all this generates suffering.

2. **The events of life** – Illness, loss, economic difficulties... they are part of human fragility.

3. **Our own choices** – Sometimes, without realizing it, we get into trouble with our decisions.

But God?

God **does not send us** the cross, but **helps us to carry it**.

Jesus himself did not seek suffering. In the Garden of Olives he prayed:

"Father, if possible, take this cup away from me. However, not mine, but your will be done." (Matthew 26:39)

When he understood that the cross was the only way to save humanity, **he accepted it out of love**.

And so we too are called to **live as saved, not as victims of suffering**.

THE EXPERIENCE OF GOD'S LOVE

To live the cross with faith, we must first of all **experience God's love.**

A small exercise that I learned and that helped me a lot is this:

1. Find a quiet place.

2. Place yourself in the presence of God.

3. Slowly repeat this phrase: **"God is a good Father who loves me."**

4. Repeat it again, with an open heart.

After a while you will feel an **inner warmth, a peace, a tenderness** that envelops you.

This is the experience of God's love.

A real, concrete, healing love.

CHANGING GOD'S VIEW

Many of us grew up with a misconception of God:

- A judge God, severe, ready to punish.

- A distant, cold, inaccessible God.

- A God who imposes laws and rules, without love.

But **this is not the God of Jesus.**

Jesus revealed to us a **God the Father**, a God who calls us by name, who loves us **with eternal love**.

The Bible says it clearly:

"Now thus saith the Lord who created you... I called you by name, you belong to me... you are worthy of esteem and I love you... do not be afraid, for I am with you." (Isaiah 43:1-6)

"I love you with eternal love, for this I still pity you." (Jeremiah 31:3)

God did not create us to make us suffer, but to make us live in love.

And even if the cross is part of our lives, **it is never the last word.**

The last word is **resurrection.** The last word is **the victory of love.**

So, if you're going through a difficult time today, remember one thing:

You're not alone.

God is with you. It supports you. He loves you.

And it will turn your pain into glory.

Chapter 8

Alice's return and the beginning of the new journey

After almost a year apart, Alice and I saw each other again.

That separate time had been necessary. I was immersed in an intense path of discernment with the priest who was helping me to understand **the deep root of my problems, my anxieties and perhaps even my vocation**. Alice, for her part, was making her own way, seeking God with all her heart, far from me but always close in faith.

The meeting happened almost by chance, but we both knew that in God's plan **chance does not exist**.

We talked for a long time. There were so many things to clarify, so many knots left unresolved, too many unanswered questions. So we decided to leave together for a journey, an experience that could help us put our hearts and our lives in order.

The destination? **Assisi.**

ASSISI, THE BEGINNING OF A NEW ROAD

It was not a place chosen at random. My first prayer group was called **"The Stigmata of St. Francis",** and in that name there was already a sign, a deep bond with that extraordinary saint who had renounced everything to follow Christ.

Assisi was the perfect place to start again.

Anyone who has had the grace to walk through its streets knows that there is something unique there. **It is as if the presence of St. Francis were still alive, as if his spirit walked with you, spoke to your heart, led you by the hand towards God.**

I felt peace. I felt the holiness that permeated the air, that spoke through the ancient stones, through the churches, through the nature that surrounded the city.

But something was wrong.

AN INVISIBLE STRUGGLE

Every morning I woke up with a **strange malaise**.

I was tired, disturbed by undefined symptoms that I could not explain. An oppressive weight crushed my soul. It almost seemed as if a dark force wanted to prevent me from enjoying that experience of peace and grace.

But then, inexplicably, in the afternoon I felt better. I was able to go to Mass, to walk the streets of Assisi, to visit the holy places.

It was as if a battle was being fought **inside me**.

And I still didn't understand its scope.

THE RETURN TO TURIN: HELL BEGINS

When I returned to Turin, everything fell apart.

All those symptoms, that indefinite malaise that I had felt in Assisi, exploded with even greater violence.

It was no longer me.

It was as if something had broken inside me, as if a wave of **darkness** had overwhelmed me. Every day was a struggle not to sink, not to let myself be annihilated.

And just in that difficult moment, Alice came back into my life in a more concrete way.

We were not back together, **but we were again traveling companions and faith**.

We supported each other, we sought God together, without labels, without definitions. **Just two wounded souls on the way to the light.**

And just in those days, Alice left for a special meeting.

RIMINI: THE ENCOUNTER WITH GRACE

Alice was in Rimini for the great annual meeting of the **Renewal in the Holy Spirit**.

Those who know these encounters know how powerful they are. Thousands of people from all over Italy gather to live an experience of **prayer, healing, praise and intense preaching**.

You can breathe the presence of God.

We are witnessing recoveries.

We hear testimonies that transform the heart.

And right there, **something extraordinary happened**.

During an intercessory prayer, a charismatic priest spoke under the inspiration of the Holy Spirit and said:

"The Lord is entering the lives of two people. He will intervene and resolve their situation."

Alice heard these words, and knew, **without any doubt, that they referred to us**.

He called me immediately, his heart overflowing with emotion:

"You must know that God wants to intervene in our history. Something big is about to happen."

And at that moment, a new hope ignited within me.

A MEETING THAT CHANGED EVERYTHING

Almost at the same time as Alice's experience in Rimini, I met a couple who were part of the **Renewal in the Holy Spirit**.

I won't name names, but **I'm sure it was God who put them in my way**.

When we started talking, I was shocked.

They told me their story and it was as **if they were talking about my life**. They too had been facing a **huge spiritual struggle** for years, with symptoms and experiences similar to mine.

I listened to them with a heart in turmoil, unable to believe what I heard.

And then came the sentence that changed everything:

"Brother, yours are not just psychological problems. Medicine can do a lot, but not everything. Sometimes, certain battles are not fought with medicines, but with the weapons of the spirit."

My blood froze.

I had always looked for answers in doctors, specialists, human paths.

But now, for the first time, someone was telling me that my **problem had a deep spiritual root**.

They said to me with love and firmness:

"You have to go to an exorcist priest. A spiritual consultation could be an eye-opener."

I was speechless.

Was it possible that what I was experiencing was something bigger than me?

That evil was trying to destroy me because God had a powerful plan for my life?

THE MOMENT OF TRUTH

I had never seriously thought about this possibility.

Yet, that evening, while I was praying, I felt a very strong urge inside me. **I had to do something.**

I had **to face the truth**, whatever it was.

My story was taking an unpredictable turn. And I had no idea what awaited me.

But one thing I knew: **God was with me.**

And that was enough.

CHAPTER 9

The spiritual journey with an exorcist

I still remember very clearly the day when, for the first time in my life, I came into contact with an **exorcist**.

Until then, my vision of this figure had been filtered by films, by the stories of others, by images that were often stereotyped. But that day reality collided with my imagination. **And it was a strong impact.**

The exorcist who welcomed me was an elderly man, but with a light in his eyes that spoke of dedication, experience, love for one's neighbor. **He was a man of God, a priest with a mission as difficult as it was necessary.**

Many priests are fleeing from this ministry. **He didn't.**

He said to me with a serene smile:

"God has called me to serve souls who suffer. This is my place, my vocation."

There was no fear in him, there was no hesitation. **Only love, only obedience to God.**

That day I was not alone. **The couple of the Renewal who had guided me to him were with me. And Alice was there too.**

Anchovy...

His presence surprised and moved me. She could have stayed away, looked at everything from the outside. But no. It was there. **And only God knows what strength He had given her to face such a difficult journey alongside me.**

I will never forget it. **Never.**

DISCERNMENT: A FRIGHTENING TRUTH

Getting to an exorcist is no small thing. The Church has a **precise and rigorous process** to discern the real cases of infestation or spiritual vexation. **If this were not the case, every exorcist priest would be overwhelmed with requests.**

Yet, I had passed every filter. **There was something about me that couldn't be explained by psychology or medicine alone.**

The priest listened to me attentively. **He scrutinized my gaze, my words, my own breathing.**

Then he said very sweetly:

"Son, we will begin with prayer. And we'll see."

Everything seemed normal, but something happened.

While the priest prayed over me, I felt an **unbearable weight inside**, a sense of **deep oppression**, almost as if something inside me was stirring and did not want to be there.

My body reacted even before my mind.

Coming out of that meeting, I felt **dizzy, confused, with an excruciating headache.**

And then something happened that shocked me: **I spat out holy water.**

They asked me to drink it. It was just water. It had no taste, it had nothing special. **Yet for me it was unbearable.**

My throat closed, my stomach rebelled. **I tasted horrible, disgusting, like rotten meat.**

Because?

It was a sign.

One of those signs that **cannot be ignored**.

The elderly priest nodded earnestly and said:

"We will continue. This is just the beginning."

THE PATH OF LIBERATION: AN EXPERIENCE BEYOND THE IMAGINABLE

From that day, **my life changed completely**.

My path to liberation had begun.

And it would not have been easy.

Once a month I went back to him. Every encounter was a battle, every prayer revealed something more.

The first few months were hell.

Everything I had inside, everything that had tormented me, **began to come out with indescribable violence**.

Uncontrollable tears, **tears for no reason**, a sense of anguish that left me no respite.

I wanted to escape.

"That's it, I don't want to come here anymore!"

I often said that. But then, each time, I found the strength to come back.

And the more I returned, the more the evil stirred inside me.

It was as if **an invisible war was being fought in my spirit**.

And in the meantime, my daily life had become a nightmare.

NIGHTS WITHOUT PEACE, DAYS OF SUFFERING

In the first months of the journey with the exorcist, my symptoms worsened frighteningly.

I lived my days **in a sort of deep coma**, as if I was no longer myself.

I slept for hours and hours during the day, **but at night... At night I didn't sleep a wink.**

And when I managed to fall asleep, **I woke up in absurd positions**, as if someone had moved me.

The pains in the body were excruciating. **Stabbing.**

Every day I vomited. **Every day.**

The fears inside me were amplified to the nth degree. **I was a living puppet.**

I didn't remember anything.

"You spoke to me yesterday!"

They told me. But **I didn't remember anything. It was no longer me.**

Yet, despite everything, **God gave me the strength to go to Mass every day. Every day.**

Even if it was **an ordeal**.

Even if I came home destroyed, **annihilated**.

Only when I went to the **exorcist** did I feel a relief, however brief it was.

THE ANSWERS I WAS LOOKING FOR

Gradually, **everything began to become clear**.

What had happened to me that evening with Alessandra?

Who was Alessandra really?

Why had my life been plunged into a vortex of pain from that moment?

Why had the symptoms come back stronger and stronger?

At every meeting with the exorcist, at every prayer, **the pieces of the puzzle came together**.

The journey was **very long, painful, exhausting**.

But **God healed my every wound**.

God freed me **from all the evil that had chained me**.

It was a real path of liberation.

A journey that I would not wish on anyone.

But today, **if I am the person I am, it is also thanks to that path**.

SPIRIT AND PSYCHE: A NECESSARY BALANCE

On my way, I also learned another important lesson.

The Church always advises, in these cases, to combine spiritual liberation with a psychological path.

Because spiritual evil can **also affect the mind, the heart, the emotions**.

Both must be treated.

And so I did.

It was a long journey, **but in the end the light won over darkness**.

God won.

And I **am here to testify to it.**

CHAPTER 10
The mystery of curses: reality or suggestion?

We live in a world dominated by science, progress and rationality. Today everything seems to be able to be explained with formulas, research and studies. **Yet, there is an invisible dimension, a shadow that moves silently between the folds of our existence, a reality that many deny but which is increasingly evident to those who are victims of it: the power of curses.**

The belief that it is possible to cast a curse on someone is as old as man. **In every culture and religion, we have always spoken of people capable of using evil to strike others.** Hatred, envy, jealousy... Human feelings that, if taken to the extreme, become lethal weapons, not only psychologically, but also spiritually.

But what is a curse? Is it just autosuggestion, a legacy of archaic beliefs, or is there really a dark force capable of breaking people's lives?

The answer is clear for those who have experienced it on their own skin.

THE POWER OF EVIL WORDS AND INTENTIONS

Curses are not just formulas spoken in a moment of anger. **They are real acts of spiritual destruction**, in which a person, driven by the desire to harm, seeks the help of occult forces to achieve a devastating effect on another person or an entire family.

"There are no effective remedies, so we think of unnatural causes."

When a person sees his life crumble for no apparent reason, when medicine cannot explain certain sudden illnesses, when everything you try to build is destroyed for no reason... Then **you begin to suspect that there is something more.**

Mysterious illnesses, broken relationships, ruined careers, unexplained accidents... Are they just unfortunate coincidences? Or is there something deeper behind it?

THE CURSE AND ITS LINK WITH THE DEVIL

One cannot speak of curses without talking about **Satan and his work in the world**.

Saint Paul warns us that **our struggle is not against creatures of flesh and blood, but against principalities and powers, against the rulers of this world of darkness, against the spirits of evil who dwell in the heavenly regions** (Ephesians 6:12).

Evil acts in many ways, but its goal is always the same: **to distance man from God**.

Curses are one of the tools with which the devil tries **to make life impossible for people**, leading them to despair, loss of faith, total destruction.

What many modern priests and theologians today tend to ignore, **was instead clear for the early Church**.

Paul VI himself forcefully stated:

"The evil that exists in the world is not only a deficiency, but a living, spiritual, perverse and perverting being. A dark enemy and enemy number one."

And John Paul II reiterated:

"He who does not believe in the existence of the devil does not believe in the Gospel."

The devil can act with subtle temptations, but also with **vexations, oppression and possessions**.

And **the curse is one of his most subtle and destructive weapons**.

THE SYMPTOMS OF A CURSE: WHEN LIFE BECOMES HELL

Many people who live under the influence of a curse **don't even know they are**.

The symptoms can be the most varied:

- Sudden and incurable diseases, not explainable by science.

- Inexplicable depression and despair.

- Panic attacks, irrational fears and perennial anxiety.

- Terrifying nightmares, with the feeling of being touched or dragged into sleep.

- Mental confusion, difficulty concentrating, memory loss.

- Inexplicable impediments in life: blocks in study, work, marriage.

- Continuous accidents, sudden breakdowns of relationships without an apparent logic.

- Rejection of sacred things: difficulty in praying, annoyance with sacred images, inability to enter the church.

These symptoms **are not the result of suggestion**, as many tend to think. **These are experiences lived every day by thousands of people.**

And those who have tried them **know that these are not coincidences.**

I myself **have experienced almost all of these symptoms**.

"I can assure you that your life is being turned into hell. You can't live like this!"

Yet, if the Lord allowed all this, **it was for a greater good**.

DELIVERANCE: THE ONLY TRUE CURE COMES FROM GOD

Once a curse has been recognized, **the real question is: how do you get out of it?**

The answer is only one: **Christ is the only true way of liberation.**

No white magic, no new age ritual, no human remedy can ever break the chains of evil. **Only Jesus Christ has the power to overcome the devil.**

For this reason the Church, **instituted by Christ for the salvation of humanity**, has received the power to free souls from the chains of the evil one.

"In my name they will cast out demons" (Mark 16:17).

"I have given you power to walk over serpents and scorpions and over all the power of the enemy" (Luke 10:19).

THE POWER OF THE CHURCH AND THE SACRAMENTS

God did not leave his children at the mercy of evil. **He gave us very powerful weapons to fight him.**

- **Prayer and fasting**, as Jesus himself taught us: *"This kind of demon can only be cast out by prayer and fasting" (Matthew 17:21).*

- **Confession**, which destroys sin and takes away the devil's power.

- **The Eucharist**, the greatest force of liberation in existence.

- **Worship and the Word of God**, breaking every chain.

- **Exorcisms and prayers of liberation**, entrusted to priests.

CONCLUSION: EVIL DOES NOT HAVE THE LAST WORD

If today the phenomenon of demonic curses and vexations is growing, it is because the world is **moving away from God**.

Yet, Christ's promise is eternal:

"I am with you always, to the close of the age" (Matthew 28:20).

Anyone who finds themselves living similar experiences **should not despair**.

Christ has already won.

The devil can torment, he can try to destroy... but **before the name of Jesus every knee bends, in heaven, on earth and under the earth (Philippians 2:10).**

Liberation is possible.

And I am a witness to this.

CHAPTER 11

The path of liberation – Getting out of it can

Liberation from evil is not a sudden event, but a **path of inner transformation**, a spiritual battle that requires faith, perseverance and absolute trust in God. **Jesus Christ is the Victor**, the One who defeated Satan once and for all with his Cross and Resurrection. However, for those who have been struck by the snares of the evil one, for those who have experienced the suffering caused by the occult, evil spells or negative spiritual bonds, the return to full freedom requires a series of fundamental steps.

The First Decision: Returning to Christ and Renounce Evil

The first necessary act to emerge from a situation of spiritual oppression is **a radical choice of belonging to Christ**. It is not enough to desire liberation: one must **desire it with all one's heart**, **commit oneself with all one's strength** and **entrust oneself completely to God**.

initial step is **the explicit renunciation of** ...ic, occultism and all forms of connection ...ld of darkness. Anyone who wants to be ...**firmly declare** his decision to belong to Christ.

This renunciation takes place in the conscious renewal of the **Baptismal Promises**, proclaiming forcefully:

"I renounce Satan, all his works and seductions. I believe in God, the Father Almighty, in Jesus Christ, his only Son, our Lord, and in the Holy Spirit."

This profession of faith is not a simple rite, but an **act of spiritual authority** that **breaks every right** that the evil one may have had over the person. Declaring one's faith means **recognizing the Lordship of Christ**, and where Jesus reigns, evil cannot remain.

The Weapons of Liberation: The Pillars of the Spiritual Life

To strengthen this decision and prevent the evil one from acting again, the Church offers very powerful tools that **protect, purify and strengthen**.

1. Constant Prayer

Prayer is the breath of the soul, the direct connection with God. For those seeking liberation, **praying every day is crucial**. Some recommended practices are:

- **Invoke the Holy Spirit** every morning and evening, asking for light and protection.

- **Prayers of liberation and protection**, such as Psalm 91, the Lord's Prayer and the Prayer of St. Michael the Archangel.

2. The General Confession

The Sacrament of Reconciliation has the power to **erase sin and break ties with evil**. A **general confession**, in which all past falls are presented with humility and sincerity, is a decisive step on the path of liberation.

3. Holy Mass and the Eucharist

The Eucharist is Christ's **greatest gift to humanity**, the divine nourishment that gives strength and protection. Those who are under spiritual attack should **attend Mass frequently**, at least on Sundays, but if possible also **every day**.

Jesus said:

"He who eats my flesh and drinks my blood has eternal life, and I will raise him up at the last day." (Jn 6:54)

Every Communion is **a victory over Satan**, because it is Jesus himself who enters us, filling us with his light and his peace.

4. The Priestly Blessing and the Sacramentals

Receiving **a priest's blessing frequently** helps to keep evil away. In addition, **sacramentals** are powerful tools that the Church makes available for the protection of the faithful.

The Purification of the Soul: Penance and Conversion

Freeing oneself from evil does not only mean **breaking ties with the occult**, but also **purifying the heart** and **renewing one's life in Christ.**

The Church teaches that purification takes place through:

- **Fasting and renunciation** – Mortifying the body helps to strengthen the spirit.

- **Flee from occasions of sin** – To turn away from anything that can bring you back.

- **Forgiving enemies** – Forgiveness breaks the chains of hatred and revenge.

- **Perform works of mercy** – Love is the greatest healing force.

Every suffering offered to God with love becomes **an instrument of purification**. Nothing of what we live is lost if we hand it over to Christ.

How Long Does It Take to Get Out?

This is the question that many are asking. The answer is **in God's hands**. Some paths of liberation last months, others years. **God works in the times and ways that He sees as right for our spiritual growth**.

But one thing is certain: **those who persevere in the faith and do not give up will be set free**.

"The Lord is close to those who have a wounded heart, he saves the brokenhearted." (Psalm 34:19)

My journey lasted a whole year, a year of suffering, of struggles, of moments in which it seemed that everything was useless. But **Christ never abandoned me**. In the end, **the Lord healed me completely**.

The Final Victory: Jesus is Lord!

When liberation finally comes, one experiences **a profound peace**, a joy that the world cannot give. Wounds are healed, the heart is filled with the presence of God.

Those who have experienced evil and have seen the power of Christ cannot remain silent. He is called to bear witness that **JESUS IS THE LORD,** the only one who can break the chains and bring back to life.

To anyone who reads these words and is fighting against evil, I want to say: **don't give up**.

It is possible to get out of it. Christ is stronger than all darkness.

Seek Him with all your heart, and you will find true freedom.

Because the Truth will set you free. (Jn 8:32)

Chapter 12
The Truth Sets Us Free

"You will know the truth, and the truth will set you free." (John 8:32)

This promise of Jesus is a double-edged sword. The truth frees, but before it leads to light and healing, it can be a painful, frightening, even devastating passage. It is a door that opens onto abysses that we never imagined we would have to face, on hidden wounds that we thought were buried forever. Yet, only by passing through this door can one truly be free.

On my journey of liberation, discovering the truth was the hardest part. I wasn't prepared for what would emerge. Every exorcism was a battle between light and darkness, between God's will to restore me to life and the obstinacy of evil that wanted to keep me chained.

The first truth that emerged was **a blow to the heart**. Do you remember that girl I had met and who seemed like a simple acquaintance? **She was the key that brought down Pandora's box.**

Alessandra's Deception: The Grip of the Cult

During one of the exorcisms, the priest, strong in the authority of Christ, ordered the evil one to reveal the truth.

And what emerged was shocking.

Alessandra was not just a mysterious girl with a dark charm. **She was a priestess of the Church of Satan in Turin, one of the most influential figures in her sect.** His interest in me was not accidental. **He wanted to lure me, he wanted to drag me into the vortex of evil.**

When God intervened and made me choose to move away from her, Alessandra reacted with fury. **He cursed me out of jealousy and malice.**

But how did this curse come about?

Do you remember the "famous" ice cream I had with Alessandra? **It was not a simple dessert shared**

on an ordinary day. It was the means by which an occult rite was performed on me, without my having the slightest suspicion of it.

It was a rite of transfer, a method of transferring a curse to an object, to a food, to anything. And I swallowed it.

A week later, my ordeal began. Pain, anguish, inexplicable disorders. Little did I know that at that moment I had already been chained by the dark forces.

When this truth emerged, the priest understood that all my torment had been born from that rite. **From there the battle to break it began.**

Exorcism Sessions: Unimaginable Pain

The exorcisms were not moments of quiet prayer. They were **real battles**, encounters full of physical and inner suffering.

I was violent. Evil opposed it with all its might. During the first few sessions, **it took four or five people to keep me still on the ground.** I screamed in a voice that wasn't mine, **I said horrible words** that I would never have uttered in a normal state.

Sometimes they tied me to the chair, because the risk of me hurting myself or others was too high.

I finished each session **exhausted**, drained of all energy. **It took me days to recover.**

And it wasn't over.

Each new session brought new truths to light. **And the pain intensified.**

When truth emerges, it can be like a ray of light that pierces the darkness, but before it illuminates, it burns. My life, already marked by a dark curse, was faced with another shocking revelation, something beyond my comprehension.

If Alessandra's curse had already destroyed me, what I discovered about Paola was even more devastating.

The Second Wound: Another Wave of Darkness

Paola. Another name, another face that I had believed belonged to a closed chapter of my life. And instead, it was just another door wide open to evil.

His revenge was atrocious.

When the exorcist priest, with the authority of Christ, forced the evil one to speak, the truth emerged in its rawness.

Paola had not accepted that she had been left. Her pride, her anger, her thirst for revenge pushed her to perform **an act of pure evil**: she delivered me into the hands of a magician, the same one her grandmother frequented.

And he did it without me having the slightest idea.

Not only did he take me to him, but he orchestrated everything in a way that made me lose control completely.

I was **drugged**. I was **dragged** to that place. I was **tied up**. And I was **raped**.

Yes, I have to say that. I can't hide it, because the truth has to be told, however horrible it is.

I was the victim of abuse, consummated in the darkness of a cursed ritual, while my mind was clouded by substances I had never chosen to take.

The magician's assistant, a woman present in the ritual, **hurt my body and soul.** I was half dazed, unable to react, tied by my wrists on a bed.

I couldn't move. I couldn't defend myself.

I was at the mercy of evil, without the possibility of screaming for help.

When this truth emerged during the exorcism, **I broke down.**

Three days of absolute silence.

I couldn't speak. I couldn't think.

I was paralyzed by a pain that I could not even process.

Inside me, the hatred for Paola grew like an unstoppable fire. I felt betrayed, used, destroyed.

But most of all, **I felt broken.**

I was already wounded, I was already marked by Alessandra's curse... and now I discovered that another, even more terrible burden weighed on me.

Two malefics. **Two direct attacks on my soul.**

If one can already annihilate a person's life, what would the weight of two infernal chains have done to me?

I was on the Cross with Jesus.

Hatred, anger, crying, trauma... everything poured into me like a river in flood.

I felt like a finished man.

But just when we believe that there is no more hope, it is there that God intervenes.

The Spiritual Battle: Fighting for Freedom

The exorcist immediately understood the gravity of what had been done.

In addition to breaking the curse, it was necessary **to heal wounds, heal traumas, sever the spiritual bonds that kept me chained to evil.**

What followed was a battle to exhaustion.

Each exorcism became **a fierce duel**, a struggle that involved not only the priest and the evil one, but also myself.

Because the exorcist does his part, but **you have to do yours.**

I had to fight, cling to the faith with all my strength, resist attacks, persevere in prayer and the sacraments.

Without will, there is no way out of hell.

God can do everything, but he wants our "yes". He wants us to choose freedom, to trust him even when the pain is unbearable.

And I, despite everything, began to **choose Him**.

It was a journey of conversion.

Each step in suffering brought me closer to Jesus.

Alice: The Angel by My Side

But I wasn't alone.

God sent me human help, someone who would be by my side, even when I didn't deserve anything.

That person was **Alice.**

She was a beacon in the storm. He stood by me, **even when my heart was filled with hatred, even when my mouth spoke words of anger.**

He just wanted to help me. I rejected it.

She just wanted to love me as a friend, as a sister in Christ. I hated her for this.

I couldn't stand all that love.

I didn't want to accept it.

And yet, she **stayed**.

A blind man cannot see, says the Bible.

I was blind. Alice was the outstretched hand of God.

And no matter how much I rejected her, no matter how unfair I was to her, **she never left me**.

Today I know that no one else would have done what she did for me. **And I will thank her forever.**

Towards Healing: The Last Battle

As the journey went on, **I began to climb up.**

The spiritual phenomena did not stop immediately, the moments of suffering were still many, but something inside me **was changing**.

I bore the pain better.

I no longer let myself be carried away by despair.

And, above all, **I was beginning to see the light.**

It was a very long journey. **The wound was deep, the trauma enormous.**

But God had already established my healing.

We fought over every trauma, every bond, every scar of the soul, and the disease, slowly, began to give way.

God always wins.

Finally, after months and months of battle, **I passed into the final phase of my exorcism journey.**

Today, looking back, I see a path of pain, but **also of redemption.**

The truth destroyed me, but it also freed me.

And if I'm still here telling this story, **it's because Jesus won.**

"In the world you will have tribulation, but be confident: I have overcome the world." (John 16:33)

CHAPTER 13
The Power of Forgiveness That Heals

There are experiences in life that leave wounds so deep that they seem incurable. The evil suffered, the betrayal, the abuse, the loss... All this settles inside us like a silent poison, capable of wearing us down day after day. Yet, in the midst of so much pain, God has given us a powerful weapon, a key capable of untying every chain and freeing the soul from the prison of hatred and resentment: **forgiveness.**

But what is forgiveness really? And above all, how can a man wounded to the core find the strength to forgive those who destroyed him?

This is the story of my hardest battle. A struggle that was not fought with the strength of the arms, but with that of the heart.

Fight for Forgiveness: A Path of Blood and Tears

After everything I had experienced, after the harm inflicted by the people I had loved and trusted, **forgiving seemed an impossible task.**

How do you forgive those who broke your soul? How can you forget an abuse, a violence, a betrayal that has left indelible scars in your heart and mind?

It took months. Years, perhaps. **Endless tears.** Prayers stifled between sobs.

I didn't want to forgive. I couldn't forgive.

Hated.

Inside me I felt a devouring fire, a resentment that held me hostage. Even when I prayed, even when I participated in exorcisms, I felt that something inside me **did not want to give in.**

Forgiving those two girls meant accepting the pain. It meant acknowledging that the evil had been real, but that it would not have the last word.

Was I ready to do it?

No.

But God was leading me, step by step, toward a healing greater than any exorcism, more powerful than any deliverance: **the healing of the heart.**

The first key: be understanding

One day, as I reflected on all the evil I had received, the Lord put a devastating thought in my heart:

"And you? Are you sinless?"

I was paralyzed.

I? Sinner? Of course, I hadn't done anything comparable to what I had suffered, but was I really righteous before God?

Scripture speaks clearly:

"There is no righteous man, not even one. There is no one who has understanding, there is no one who seeks God. Everyone has gone astray,

everyone has become useless. There is no one who practices goodness, not even one." *(Romans 3:10-12)*

I was a sinner like everyone else. I needed forgiveness as much and more than those who had hurt me.

It was a blow to the heart. **If I myself needed mercy, by what right did I deny forgiveness to others?**

In that moment, I understood a truth that would change me forever:

"We cannot forgive if we have not first experienced forgiveness."

Only those who have experienced God's grace can truly extend it to others.

Forgiveness is Healing

Forgiveness does not mean forgetting.

Many think that in order to forgive you have to erase the wrong you have received from your memory, but this is not the case. To forgive means **to choose not to let the pain of the past govern our present and our future.**

The lack of forgiveness is a prison. It brings with it **hatred, resentment, bitterness**, feelings that slowly corrode the soul, mind and even body.

I was living proof of this.

The more I refused to forgive, the more I felt bad. Forgiveness was not a favor to those who had hurt me. Forgiveness was a **gift that God wanted to give me to free me.**

That is why the word *forgiveness* is so special. For-forgiveness. A gift that God gives to us, and that we choose to give to others.

Forgiveness is a Choice

Forgiving is not a feeling. It's not something that happens on its own, with time.

To forgive is **an act of will.**

This means that even though my heart was still broken, even though my pain was still alive, I could still **choose** to forgive.

And so one day, after a long journey of prayer and inner struggle, I made a decision before God.

I chose to forgive.

It was not a magical feeling. I didn't feel free right away.

But I had done my part. Now it was God's turn to complete the work.

The Three Stages of Forgiveness

On my journey, I discovered that forgiveness has three levels. Two are known, but the third is the one that many ignore:

1. **Forgiving others** – It is the first step, the most obvious but also the most difficult. It means

letting go of resentment towards those who have hurt us.

2. **Forgiving yourself** – We are often our own harshest judges. We blame ourselves for mistakes, for not having reacted, for having suffered. Learning to accept one's fragility is essential for healing.

3. **Forgiving God** – God is never wrong, but how many of us hold a grudge against Him in our hearts? For the prayers apparently not heard, for the pain that he allowed us to go through? This wound must also be healed.

Forgiveness That Breaks Chains

When I really started to forgive, **something changed.**

Exorcisms became more effective. My soul began to breathe. The poison inside me began to fade.

"If the Son makes you free, you will be truly free." *(John 8:36)*

Forgiveness accelerated my recovery.

I don't say this to say. It's the truth.

The spiritual ties with evil were broken. The wounds of the soul began to heal. Peace, the real one, began to take the place of hatred.

Jesus sees hearts.

He knows if forgiveness is only in words or if it really comes from the depths.

That day, when I decided to forgive with all my being, I felt something inside me break.

And for the first time in a long time, I really felt the weight fall off my shoulders.

Forgiveness had healed me.

"Father, forgive them, for they know not what they do." *(Luke 23:34)*

If Jesus could forgive those who crucified him, who am I not to forgive those who hurt me?

Chapter 14

From Contempt for Me to Acceptance

There are battles that are fought in silence, away from the eyes of those around us. They are inner wars, made up of thoughts, wounds, beliefs rooted in the depths of our soul.

I fought one of these battles every day. **The fight against myself.**

For years I had lived in a vortex of guilt, of contempt for myself, of a continuous and exhausting dissatisfaction.

I didn't like myself. I didn't accept myself. I saw myself wrong, defective, undeserving of love.

There was always a voice in my head that told me: *"You are not enough.", "You are not worthy.", "You are a failure."*

And that voice tormented me.

How many people live with this same voice whispering in their hearts, making them feel always out of place, always inadequate?

Yet, with time, with God's grace, I learned that that voice was not the truth. It was not God who spoke to me like this.

God looked at me with completely different eyes.

And that changed everything.

The Great Deception of Self-Contempt

Many people think that despising oneself is a form of humility. But this is not the case.

Humility is not saying, *"I'm useless, I'm worthless, I don't deserve love."*

This is a lie.

True humility is recognizing who we are before God: fragile, yes, sinners, yes, but also **deeply loved, chosen, desired by Him.**

When the enemy whispers to us that we are useless, that we are worthless, that we are not enough, **he is lying.**

Because the truth is different.

God tells us:

"Because you are precious in my eyes, because you are worthy of esteem and I love you." *(Isaiah 43:3)*

These words shocked me.

Could it be that I was **precious** in God's eyes? That I was **worthy of esteem**? That He **loved me**, despite everything?

It seemed impossible to me. Yet, it was the truth.

The Beginning of Healing: Accepting Ourselves as God Sees Us

The first step in accepting me was to understand that **God accepted me as I was.**

He didn't wait for me to become perfect. He didn't wait for me to stop making mistakes.

He loved me **as I was.**

Is this not perhaps the heart of the Gospel?

Christ did not come for the righteous, but for sinners. He did not choose the best, but the weakest.

God loves unconditionally. God loves because **he is love.**

And if God accepted me, who was I not to accept myself?

I began to see my worth through His eyes.

I wasn't a mistake. I was not a waste. I was not a person destined for failure.

I was **His son.** And that was enough.

The First Neighbor to Love: Myself

In the Gospel we find a fundamental commandment:

"Love your neighbor as yourself." *(Matthew 19:19)*

Many focus on the first part: *"Love thy neighbor."* But the second is just as important: **"like yourself."**

And here is a great truth: **we cannot love others if we do not first learn to love ourselves.**

How can I give love, if inside I have only contempt? How can I see beauty in others, if I see only darkness inside me?

The first neighbor I meet every day is me.

And God asks me to treat myself with the same mercy with which He treats me.

Forgive me. Accept me. Look at me with love, without judgment.

That was my biggest challenge.

Letting the Holy Spirit Do Truth

If there is anyone who knows every hidden corner of our hearts, it is the Holy Spirit.

He is **the light** that illuminates our shadows. He is **the voice** that whispers softly when everything else screams.

He guided me.

Slowly he showed me my true identity. He taught me that my value does not depend on what I have done or what I will do.

I am worth **it because I am His.**

And this value never changes.

The Holy Ghost helped me **see the truth about myself.**

To stop looking at myself with the eyes of my past. To stop judging me with the severity with which I had always treated myself.

He taught me to accept myself.

God Took Me to Africa to Teach Me Love

But the greatest revelation of this journey took place in an unexpected place: **Africa.**

God has mysterious ways. And to heal me he chose a journey, far from everything and everyone, to a land I did not know.

There, among the poorest and simplest people, **I discovered what it means to be loved unconditionally.**

I saw children with a smile on their faces, despite having nothing. I saw people hugging me without knowing who I was, just because I was a brother. I felt a human warmth that I had never felt before.

On that journey, God made me understand one fundamental thing:

"You are not loved because you are perfect. You are loved because you are mine."

And at that moment, the contempt that had poisoned my soul for years **began to fall.**

I looked in the mirror and, for the first time, **I didn't see an enemy.** I saw **a beloved son.**

And that day, something inside me changed forever.

Conclusion: Acceptance is an Act of Faith

Accepting oneself is not a feeling. It's not something that happens overnight.

It is **an act of faith.**

It is believing the Word of God more than we believe our fears. It is choosing to see ourselves with His eyes, instead of those of the world. It is to stop hating ourselves for what we are not, and to start giving thanks for what we are.

Because, in the end, the truth is only one:

"You are precious in my eyes. You are worthy of esteem. I love you." *(Isaiah 43:3)*

And if God loves us like this, who are we not to do the same?

CHAPTER 15

The Journey to Africa – The Path to Healing

There are journeys that we make with the body, others that we make with the soul. The trip to Africa was both for me.

For years I had dreamed of setting foot in that fascinating land, a place that seemed to call me, as if a part of me already belonged to those endless and wild landscapes.

I had asked God many times to grant me this experience, but I never imagined that He would take me there not only to admire the beauty of creation, but to **heal the deepest wounds of my soul.**

Yet, this is precisely how God works. When we least expect it, in the most unthinkable ways, He intervenes and transforms our hearts.

And that's what happened to me.

Africa: love at first sight

The journey lasted three weeks. Three weeks that changed my life.

As soon as I landed, I immediately felt something different in the air. It was a living, pulsating place, full of colors, smells, sounds that enveloped you.

Africa is not just a continent, it is **an experience.**

It is the sky that is ablaze with red and orange at sunset. It is the song of birds at dawn, as the savannah awakens. It is the red earth under your feet, which seems to tell ancient stories.

The first part of the journey was immersed in the beauty of creation.

I visited the **Kruger Park**, the largest wildlife park in South Africa.

Seeing the animals in their natural habitat was something indescribable.

Watching a lion move proudly, elephants advancing majesticly, giraffes stretching their necks to catch the highest leaves... It was as if nature itself was speaking to me, reminding me of God's greatness.

It was not just a journey, it was an **encounter with Creation**.

But the real miracle, the real transformation, happened in the third week.

The Encounter with Pure Love: The Children of Pemba

After two weeks in South Africa, we moved to Mozambique, to the island of **Pemba**, and there began the deepest journey, the inner one.

We went to Metoro, in the province of Cabo Delgado, to visit the **Girasol** kindergarten, a small town that welcomes children in difficulty.

I wasn't ready for what I would find.

I expected poverty, sadness, need... But I found **smiles, joy, light.**

The children had nothing, yet they were **happy.** They ran towards us, hugged us, took us by the hand as if they had always known us.

Their eyes shone with a pure, genuine joy, **a joy that depended not on what they possessed, but on what was in their hearts.**

And there, something in me began to change.

The miracle: the child who healed me

There was one day in particular that I will never forget.

I was getting off the bus, ready for a new day with the kids.

Suddenly, a small child approached me.

I didn't know his name. He had a huge smile and two big eyes that seemed to look straight into my **soul.**

Without saying anything, he took my hand.

And in that instant, **I felt something incredible.**

A voice inside me said clearly:

"Unless you become like children, you will not enter the kingdom of heaven. I will heal you." *(Matthew 18:1-5)*

It was not just any voice. It wasn't my mind.

He was **God.**

It was He who spoke to me, through that child, through that innocent gaze, through that small gesture full of love.

And in an instant, everything changed.

The Healing of My Heart

For years I had carried a deep wound inside me.

After everything that had happened with **Alessandra and Paola**, the pain had consumed me.

But it wasn't just pain.

It had become **hatred**.

Hatred towards the female world. Hatred that closed my heart. Hatred that prevented me from trusting, from opening up, from loving.

It was an invisible chain that held me prisoner.

But that day, when that child took me by the hand, **that chain broke.**

When I returned to Italy, I realized something incredible:

That hatred had disappeared.

I no longer felt resentment, I no longer felt anger, **I was free.**

God had healed me.

And it all happened with such a simple gesture: a child's hand in mine.

Forgiveness and Freedom

From that day, I began a new journey.

A path of **forgiveness**.

I forgave **Alessandra and Paola**. I forgave **myself** for allowing hatred to consume me. I forgave **the past** and let go of the pain.

It was as if God had opened a door in my soul and said to me:

"Now you are free. Now you can love again."

Conclusion: God Meets Us Where We Don't Expect Him

That trip to Africa was supposed to be just a vacation.

But God turned it into an experience of **healing, redemption, and love.**

God does not always speak to us with great signs or spectacular miracles.

Sometimes it speaks to us in silence, in the smile of a child, in a hand that holds us with love, in a journey that changes our lives.

God healed me in Africa. And He did it with the sweetness of a child, to remind me that **to enter His Kingdom, we must return to being like them.**

Small, simple, open to love.

Free.

CHAPTER 16

The Journey to Medjugorje – A Healing Stage

There are places on earth where heaven seems to touch the ground, where God's presence becomes more tangible, closer, more intense. Medjugorje is one of these places.

It was not a trip planned by me. It was my exorcist who organized it, feeling that many of us, including the people he followed in his ministry, needed a pilgrimage, a deeper encounter with divine grace.

On the bus there were not only people who, like me, struggled with spiritual and inner wounds. There were also healthy people, ordinary faithful, simple pilgrims who wanted to live a Marian experience.

For me, however, that trip would have been something more.

A turning point. One of the three stages of my complete liberation.

The journey: a traumatic journey

The journey to Medjugorje was anything but smooth.

I can't explain exactly why, but from the moment the bus started, a strange restlessness took hold of me.

It was as if there was a battle going on inside me.

A mixture of anxiety, fear and discomfort that I could not control. And I wasn't the only one.

Other people who had difficult spiritual situations also began to feel bad. Some felt nauseous, others felt an inexplicable weight on their chest, some even felt a strong agitation for no reason.

It seemed that something inside us **resisted** the idea of approaching that holy place.

The priest, who accompanied us, reassured us with words of comfort:

"It is normal for the evil one to rebel when we draw close to God. But don't worry, Jesus is waiting for us."

Those words gave me some peace, but the journey was still tiring.

Yet, despite everything, we finally arrived.

And I didn't know yet that that week would be one of the most intense of my life.

Medjugorje: A Place Where Heaven Touches Earth

As soon as I got off the bus, I felt a different air.

I don't know how to describe it, but Medjugorje has something unique.

There is a particular peace that envelops everything.

The mountains, the churches, the streets, even the people... everything seemed to be permeated by a light that was not only visible, but **spiritual**.

I looked around and, for the first time in a long time, I felt **a little hope inside me**.

The priest guided us in the first moments of prayer.

He took us to the Church of St. James, invited us to participate in Eucharistic Adoration and to walk along the **Hill of Apparitions**, the place where Our Lady appeared to the six visionaries in 1981.

Every step on that hill seemed to be a step inside myself.

Every prayer, every song, every silence seemed to dig deeper, bringing my wounds to light.

But the most important moment, the one that marked a decisive turning point in my journey, was a special meeting.

Exorcism with the Help of a Charismatic Sister

My exorcist knew a very special nun.

She was a religious with **special gifts**, a charism of discernment and intercession that had helped many people on the path of liberation.

Hearing my story, he decided to join the priest during a prayer for me.

I didn't know what was going to happen. I had no idea how difficult it would be.

But that day, during the prayer of deliverance, something inside me rebelled.

A Violent Spiritual Battle

They told me what happened, because I personally **don't remember anything**.

During the exorcism, I began to speak in languages I had never known.

I screamed, I cursed with words of incredible violence.

The anger, the fury, the resistance... everything manifested itself at that moment.

They told me it took **three men** to hold me down.

I, who had never been particularly strong physically, gave off a strength that did not seem human.

Yet, at that very moment, right in the middle of that invisible battle, **Jesus was there.**

I felt it in my heart.

Even though my mind was darkened, even though my words were of anger, deep in my spirit there was **a sweet and reassuring presence**

And after a time that seemed endless...

The darkness **broke.**

Peace After the Storm

When it was all over, I was exhausted.

My body felt heavy, as if I had run for miles without stopping.

But inside, **something had changed.**

I can't say that I was completely free at that moment, but I knew one thing for sure:

Another chain had been broken.

I felt a lightness I had never felt before.

A sense of peace that was not just emotion, but something deeper.

As if a piece of my soul had been **returned** to light.

The Return: A New Beginning

When the week in Medjugorje ended and we returned home, I was a different person.

Not that everything was resolved, not that the battle was over.

But **I felt hope**.

I felt that **Jesus had taken me by the hand**, as a father does with a wounded son.

And I felt that **the road to liberation had now almost come to an end.**

That trip was not just a pilgrimage. It was an **encounter with grace.**

Something inside me had **really changed.**

Chapter 17
The Second Total Deliverance from the Evil One

There are times in life when you feel that a battle has come to an end. After months, perhaps years, of struggle, of darkness, of fear, the day comes when light definitively wins over darkness.

My journey towards inner freedom and spiritual healing was not immediate, but marked by precise stages, moments in which God worked in me with incredible power.

The first big turning point came in **Medjugorje**, that holy place where the evil inside me began to lose its power. But, as often happens in the spiritual path, the struggle did not end there.

It was as if God had opened a breach in my soul, letting His light in, but the enemy still resisted. I felt that my liberation **was not yet complete**.

Then, that day in October came, when everything changed forever.

Meeting with a Charismatic Preacher

After Medjugorje, I returned to my Renewal in the Spirit group. It was summer, and within the group a meeting had been organized with a charismatic preacher, a man of faith recognized for his spiritual gifts.

His name was **Massimo Coero Borga**, founder of the community **"The Risen Crucifix"**. A man who had dedicated his life to preaching the Gospel with the power of the Holy Spirit, bringing liberation and healing to so many wounded souls.

I didn't know yet that that meeting would be **decisive** for me.

That day, Maximus preached with great authority, speaking of God's love, the power of the Holy Spirit, and Christ's victory over death and sin.

His every word penetrated my heart like a sharp blade, tearing through the last resistances that the enemy still had within me.

I felt that God was preparing **something great**.

The Healing Prayer and the Moment of Truth

After the preaching, Maximus invited everyone to pray together, asking the Lord to come down with His power and free anyone who was still oppressed by evil.

I wasn't sure what to expect.

I had already experienced moments of struggle, of partial liberation, but this time something inside me told me that God was about to complete His work.

When Maximus began to pray for those present, the Holy Spirit began to move forcefully in the room.

Some people cried, others fell to the ground overwhelmed by God's love.

Then it was my turn.

The Final Battle

When Massimo laid his hands on me and began to pray, I immediately felt a reaction inside me.

It was as if something **was fighting not to go out**.

My body stiffened, a dark force tried to resist, but the Holy Spirit was stronger.

Then, suddenly, **it happened**.

I heard a scream **come out of me**, something that came off violently, as if an invisible chain were suddenly broken.

My body collapsed to the ground, exhausted.

It took **two or three people** to help me get up.

And when I finally got back on my feet, **everything had changed**.

I looked around and saw the eyes of one of my brothers in the group fixed on me.

He smiled at me and said to me, in a firm but joyful voice:

"It's time to celebrate, now here we are!"

Those words were **prophetic**.

It was really over.

Evil no longer had any power over me.

The battle was over.

I was **free**.

Liberation Day: 18 October 2015

It was a day I will never forget.

After almost **a year of struggle**, after suffering, battles, exorcisms, moments of despair and moments of light, **I was finally reborn**.

It was Sunday **18 October 2015**.

A day that I will always mark in my heart as the day **when God gave me back my life**.

My soul had been purified. The chains had been broken. Christ had won in me.

The Signs of Rebirth

In the following days, everything in my life **visibly changed**.

For the first time in a long time:

I slept **very well**, without nightmares, without disturbances, without nocturnal oppression. I felt **full of strength**, as if a new energy pervaded me. I even began to regain **weight**, which had always been difficult for me.

My mind was **free**, with no more obsessions, no more negative thoughts. I saw **life opening up in front of me**, like a road finally clear.

It was a new, **different, profound** normality.

It was **true freedom**.

The Confirmation of Healing

Day by day, that peace continued to grow.

It was not a passing emotion, it was not something momentary.

It was a **true inner transformation**.

After a long time, my heart was light.

I was healed.

I felt it inside me, with a certainty that no one could take away from me.

It was the greatest confirmation that God had performed His miracle in me.

And from that day, everything was different.

From that day, my life really started again.

CHAPTER 18
The Third Final Healing

There are experiences in life that mark a before and an after. There are times when the soul perceives with absolute certainty that God has acted, that His work is done.

After the trip to Medjugorje and the final liberation with the prayer of the charismatic preacher, I felt a peace inside me that I had never felt before. There were no more torments, no nightmares, no more oppression. For the first time in a long time, I felt **free**.

But the definitive confirmation of this healing, God's ultimate seal on this path, would come a few months later, at a time I **could never have** imagined.

The Return to the Exorcist: The Verification of Liberation

I knew that, after everything I had experienced, I would have to return to the exorcist priest who had followed me on that long path of spiritual struggle.

It was not an obligation, but a verification.

I wanted to share my healing with him, to tell him how God had completed His work in me.

And so, accompanied by my father and some people who had lived through this battle with me – including a psychiatrist who followed several similar cases and who knew me well – I went to the meeting.

The exorcist welcomed me with his usual attentive gaze. He knew that moment would be important.

We started with prayer.

The Moment of Confirmation: The Light of Glory

During previous exorcisms, my body always reacted with strong resistance. There was closure, there was struggle, there was a darkness that opposed the light of God.

But this time, **everything was different.**

As the exorcist prayed, I felt a deep peace. There was no negative reaction, no malaise, no feeling of oppression.

I was free.

But it was at that moment that something **absolutely extraordinary** happened, something I will never forget.

Suddenly, **a vision opened up before my eyes**.

It was as if the veil between heaven and earth had been lifted for an instant, and I could see beyond the material world.

An immense, almost dazzling light **appeared in front of me**.

It was such a bright light that I should have looked away, but at the same time it was sweet, welcoming, full of love.

And inside that light, behind each of the people who were with me in that room, **I saw wonderful figures appear**. They were **the Saints**.

They were not images carved in marble or painted on ancient canvases, **they were alive**.

And the thing that struck me most was that **they were young**.

It was as if time had no power over them, as if they lived in an eternal beauty, a beauty that never fades away, that never grows old.

At that moment I understood that every person in that room was **accompanied** by the Saint to whom she was most devoted, the one who in life or death had interceded for her.

And among them I also recognized the Saints who, during the long months of spiritual battle, had intervened to help me overcome evil.

It was a vision **of glory, of victory, of light**.

And a voice that was clear, sweet and powerful at the same time, resounded in my heart, a voice that I knew came from God:

"It's really over. You're healed."

In that instant, I knew that God was putting **His final seal** on my healing.

There was nothing more to fear.

There was nothing left to fight.

The battle was over.

God had won.

The Encounter with the Supernatural: An Unexpected Gift

After the vision, I remained silent for a few moments.

I was overwhelmed with emotion, with joy, with the awareness of what I had just seen.

The exorcist, noticing my state, looked at me with a smile full of peace and said words that I still carry in my heart today:

"When a soul is completely liberated, something extraordinary always happens."

I could only nod, because what I had experienced was beyond any possible explanation.

It was **a gift**.

A rare gift, which God had chosen to grant me **to seal my healing**, to show me with absolute certainty that **evil no longer had any power over me**.

And I could only thank him.

To thank him for every past suffering. Thank him for every tear shed. To thank him for every battle fought. Because **in everything, He had been with me**.

And now, His victory was my victory.

The Certainty of Healing: A New Beginning

From that day, **nothing was the same as before**.

My life had **totally changed**.

Not only did I no longer have any sign of spiritual oppression, but I had a new awareness of who I was.

I was **a child of God**. I was **free**. I was **deeply loved** by the Lord.

Fear was no longer part of me.

I no longer lived in doubt, in uncertainty, in the shadow of the past.

I had seen with my own eyes the reality of the sky. I had heard God's voice with my heart.

And there was no more room for fear.

It was the time of joy.

It was the time to **really live**, without chains, without any more wounds, without the weight of evil.

God had made **all things new**.

And from that day, my life **really began**.

CHAPTER 19
God is Love that Saves

Life is a journey. Sometimes, that journey takes us to dark places, uncertain roads, moments of trial. But if there is one truth that I have understood deeply, after my long journey of liberation, it is this: **God is love!**

Not an abstract love, not a philosophical concept or a cliché to be repeated in church. No. **God is concrete, living, real love. It is a love that heals, transforms, renews. It is a love that saves.**

A love that comes together

All of us, at least once in our lives, have heard: **"God is love."**

But the question is: **Do we really believe it? Have we experienced it?**

For a long time I said it too, perhaps out of habit, perhaps because I heard it repeated. But only when I crossed the path of liberation could I **truly encounter His love**.

God did not reveal himself to me in a single instant, it was not a sudden love at first sight. He made himself known **slowly**, step by step, freeing me from my wounds, my pride, my inner chains.

The encounter with God was not only an emotional experience, but a profound transformation, which touched every part of my life. **Nothing has remained the same as before.**

When you meet true love, you change.

God loves us as we are... But it doesn't leave us as we are

Today, one of the most widespread slogans in the world is this:

"God loves us just as we are."

And it's true! **God's love is unconditional.**

But there is another fundamental aspect that we often forget:

God loves us too much to leave us as we are!

God's love is not passive, it is not a love that merely accepts us and leaves us in our weaknesses. **It is a love that transforms, that makes us grow, that shapes us as a potter does with clay.**

Every trial we experience, every season of our life, every difficulty and every joy are instruments in God's hands to form us, to make us **become more and more like him**.

We will never be the same.

If we walk with God, every day we will be different, more mature, stronger, more filled with His love.

God's Love is Different from the Love of the World

We live in a world that talks a lot about love, but often doesn't know true love.

In the world, love is often conditional:

- **If you respond to the expectations of others, then you are loved.**

- **If you meet certain standards, then you are accepted.**

- **If you're useful, then you're worth something.**

But God is not like that.

God **does not love us for what we do, he does not love us for what we can offer him.**

He loves us because he has chosen to love us.

A love that precedes all our merits

God's Word tells us:

"We love because He loved us first." *(1 John 4:19)*

And again:

"For while we were yet without strength, Christ died in due time for the wicked. Hardly would anyone die for a righteous man; but perhaps for a good person someone would have the courage to die. But God shows the greatness of his love for us in this: that while we were still sinners, Christ died for us." *(Romans 5:6-8)*

God has always loved us.

When we were weak, when we were lost, when we were far from Him... **He already loved us.**

If God's love were based on our own merits, it would be an unstable love.

We change, we waver, we make mistakes. If God loved us only when we were "good," then His love would be as uncertain as we are.

But **God is constant. God is faithful.**

God never changes in His love for us!

God is Love, but Not Just Any Love

Today there is a lot of talk about God as love, but often a distorted image is made of him.

God is not a love that justifies everything, that turns a blind eye to sin, that leaves us in our mediocrity.

God is **a love that saves**, a love **that leads to holiness**, a love **that desires the best for us, not the bare minimum.**

God **cannot** fail to love us.

Love is His essence. **He is pure, perfect, eternal love.**

And His greatest desire is **to have a loving relationship with us.**

Not a religion, not a set of rules, but a living and true relationship.

Like a father with his son. Like a friend with a friend. Like a groom with his bride.

Man Is Capable of Loving Because He Was Created to Love

We were created in the image and likeness of God.

And if God is love, then **we too were created to love**.

We have this wonderful ability in our hearts: **to receive love and to give love**.

But until we understand **God's love for us**, we will never be able to live true love.

Because **only those who feel loved can truly love**.

Only those who have experienced **unconditional, faithful, eternal love** can stop looking for in others what only God can give.

Conclusion: A Renewed Life in God's Love

If there is one thing I have learned on this journey, it is that **God changes lives**.

His love is not an idea, it is not a philosophy, it is not a theory.

It is **power that** transforms.

Today I am a different person. Today **I know that I am loved, I know that I am a child of God.** Today **I know that His love will never leave me**.

And this is the greatest certainty that a man can have.

God is love that saves. And if you let him into your life, your story will never be the same.

Let yourself be loved by him. Let yourself be transformed. Let us save you.

Because **only in the love of God can true life be found.**

Chapter 20

The Discovery of God's Love and the Outpouring of the Holy Spirit

There are truths that we touch on, concepts that we have always heard, but that only at a certain moment in our lives affect us deeply and change everything.

For me, one of these truths was this: **God suffers for us.**

It is not a question of a distant, detached God, insensitive to our choices. No, the God I have met is **a loving Father, a most tender Father, a Father who grieves when His children turn away from Him.**

God Suffers for Our Sin

This was a shocking discovery for me.

We often think of God as the One who punishes, who judges, who waits for the moment when He can make us pay for our mistakes.

But the reality is **exactly the opposite.**

God does not rejoice in seeing us suffer. God does not desire our ruin. God does not want to lose us.

When we fall into sin, it **is He who suffers**. When we drift away, it **is He who is saddened**. When we ignore Him, **it is He who grieves**.

Not because He is a fragile God, but because **He truly loves us.**

And true love is that which suffers for the loved one.

God's heart beats for each one of us. We are not numbers before Him, we are not part of an indistinct mass. **Each of us is of immense value in His eyes.**

That is why **when we remain indifferent to His love, we do Him an immense wrong**.

Let us think of a father who loves his child, who takes care of him, who supports him, who helps him... and that son ignores him, treats him coldly, walks away.

How can that father not suffer?

Here, this is God.

God **wants the best for us, even when life puts us to the test.** Even when we are called to carry the cross, he is there, close, he supports us, he guides us, he loves us.

The Beginning of My True Conversion

There is a phrase that marked me deeply:

**"Now thus saith the Lord who created you... I have called you by name, you belong to me, you are worthy of esteem and I love you. Do not be afraid, for I am with you." —*Isaiah 43:1-6*.

These words are not only beautiful. **They are true.**

God **knows me by name.** God **chose me.** God **loves me, not because I deserve it, but because He is Love.**

Here my true conversion began.

Not when I started going to Mass more often. Not when I have improved my behavior. Not when I have eliminated certain sins from my life.

My conversion began when I began to listen to His voice and respond with a sincere heart.

And I understood something fundamental: **conversion is not a moment, it is a journey.**

The Danger of Self-Belief

Before this revelation, I had fallen into a subtle but dangerous trap:

I thought I was already converted.

- I went to Mass.

- Pray.

- I did not commit great sins.

So I was already good to go, wasn't I?

How many times do we hear this phrase: **"I am already converted."**

But this is a great illusion!

We **are not converted**, we **are on the way to conversion**.

Every day we have to ask ourselves:

- **Am I growing in faith or am I still?**

- Am I letting God transform my life?

- Am I allowing grace to change my heart?

Conversion **is an ongoing process. It is fatigue, it is struggle, it is daily choice.**

The Shift in Perspective: Discovering the True Face of God

Another mistake I made was the vision I had of God.

For a long time I had seen him **as a strict master**, who imposed laws, who demanded obedience, who punished those who made mistakes.

But **when you meet true love, your vision changes**.

God **is not a master**. God **does not impose** anything. God **does not force anyone to love him**.

God **puts himself at our service**.

God **sent His Son Jesus to the cross for us**.

He gave His life for me, He gave His life for you.

How could he not love us?

The Outpouring of the Holy Spirit: A New Birth

A few months after I had begun to feel better, within the Renewal of the Spirit group to which I belonged, I received **the outpouring of the Holy Spirit**.

What is the outpouring of the Holy Spirit?

In simple words, **it is an intense prayer, made by a Christian community, that the Holy Spirit may descend abundantly on those who desire it with all their heart.**

It is not a sacrament, but is closely linked to the sacraments of **Baptism and Confirmation**.

In practice, **it revives and renews our relationship with God**.

When the Holy Spirit **takes possession of a believer's life, something changes.**

But for this to happen, **one must be willing to open one's heart.**

- **The Holy Spirit does not enter those who close the door to him.**

- **The Holy Spirit does not force anyone.**

- **The Holy Spirit acts only in those who abandon themselves to Him.**

And that day **I abandoned myself completely.**

A completely transformed life

After that experience, **my life was never the same.**

It wasn't just a matter of emotions. It was not just a time of spiritual fervor. **It was a real inner transformation.**

God **had become the center of my life.** It was no longer an idea, a doctrine, a religion.

He was my Father. He was my Savior. It was my Everything.

Conclusion: A New Birth in Christ

If I had to sum it all up in one sentence, I would say this:

That day I was reborn.

As Scripture says:

"If anyone is in Christ, he is a new creation; old things have passed away; behold, all things have become new." *(2 Corinthians 5:17)*

And this is the wonder of Christian life: **we are never still.**

If we let God act, **every day will be a day of growth, of conversion, of renewal.**

My story does not end here. Because **the journey with God never ends.**

And I know one thing: **today I am closer to Him than yesterday. And tomorrow I will be even more so.**

Because **God is Love. A Love that never ceases to transform those who let themselves be loved.**

CHAPTER 21

The New Identity in Christ

If there is one question that every human being asks himself, in one way or another, it is this: **Who am I really?**

It is a profound, essential question that marks the entire journey of life.

As we grow up, we hear a thousand voices trying to answer for us:

- **You are what you do.**

- **You are your success.**

- **You are your failures.**

- **You are what others say about you.**

- **You are the sum of your experiences.**

But is this really the case? **Does our identity come down to this?**

No, because there is **a bigger, truer, more authoritative voice** than all the others.

The voice of God.

And only He has the right to tell us who we really are.

The Identity Crisis of the Modern World

If we look around us, we see a world full of people who **no longer know who they are**.

We live in an age where everything is changeable, unstable, confused.

Many seek their identity in what they own:

- **In money.**

- **In success.**

- **In physical appearance.**

- **In social media.**

- **In fame, in titles, in power.**

But what happens when these things are lacking? If you've built your identity on money, who are you when you lose it? If you've built your identity on fame, who are you when others stop applauding you? If you have built your identity on your work, who are you when you retire?

That's why so many people feel lost, empty, aimless.

They looked for their identity in the wrong places.

The lies we believed

From an early age, **we have heard many lies about who we are**.

- "You're worth nothing."

- "You're not good enough."

- "You're a failure."

- "Your past defines you."

- "You'll never change."

These words, repeated, enter the heart and **build a wrong image of ourselves**.

But **the truth is different**.

We are not what people say about us. We are not our mistakes. We are not our wounds.

You may have lived through difficult moments, you may have been hurt, betrayed, rejected. But **you are not your pain. You are much more.**

And only God can tell you who you really are.

The New Identity in Christ

God's Word tells us something wonderful:

"If anyone is in Christ, he is a new creation; Old things have passed away. Behold, all things have become new." *(2 Corinthians 5:17)*

This is the truth!

If you are in Christ, you are no longer the person you were before.

- **You are no longer defined by your past.**

- **You are no longer tied to your old fears.**

- **You are no longer a slave to your sins.**

If you are in Christ, you are a new creature!

How many times do we look in the mirror and ask ourselves: **"Who am I really?"**

But **true identity is not the one we see with our eyes, it is the one that God has placed within us.**

God **has imprinted His image on us**, and this image has been restored in Christ.

We are no longer **lost, wounded, crushed by the weight of sin**. We are **children of God, loved, chosen, redeemed by the blood of Jesus.**

"God chose us before the creation of the world, to participate in divine life and become His children." *(Ephesians 1:4-5)*

This is our true identity!

Life hidden in God

If we say that we have accepted Christ as our Savior, it means that **our life is hidden in God**.

What a beautiful image!

To be hidden in God is to be safe. It means having a **refuge** where our heart finds peace.

The world offers us a thousand distractions, it pushes us to seek confirmation in material things. But those who are in Christ **no longer need to look elsewhere**.

His joy **does not depend on the things of this world**. Its value **does not come from men**. Its purpose **is not set by society**.

His life is firm in Jesus.

Those who are in Christ **have a new perspective**.

- **He is not concerned with earthly things, but with things above.**

- He does not seek human glory, but the glory of God.

- He does not live to accumulate, but to give.

And above all, **he is no longer of the world, even if he lives in the world.**

"If you have risen with Christ, seek the things that are above, where Christ is seated at the right hand of God." *(Colossians 3:1)*

Walking According to the Spirit

When we live according to our old nature, we follow **the works of the flesh:**

- **Fornication**

- **Impurity**

- **Idolatry**

- **Envy**

- **Jealousy**

- **Drunkenness**

- **Discordie**

All these things **destroy our souls and lead us away from the Kingdom of God.**

But when we live by the Spirit, our hearts are transformed.

"The fruit of the Spirit is love, joy, peace, patience, kindness, goodness, faithfulness, meekness, self-control." *(Galatians 5:22-23)*

Those who are in Christ **leave behind the old way of life** and walk in the light of the Holy Spirit.

It doesn't mean we'll never fall. But it means that **every time we fall, we get up again with God's strength.**

And the more we allow ourselves to be transformed by the Spirit, the freer , **purer, and more loving our hearts become.**

Conclusion: The Truth That Liberates

We live in a world that tells us who we should be. But **only God can tell us who we really are.**

We **are not our past.** We **are not our fears.** We **are not our failures.** We **are children of God, redeemed by the blood of Christ, loved from all eternity.**

And he who lives in this truth **walks in freedom.**

"You will know the truth, and the truth will set you free." *(John 8:32)*

This is our identity. This is our certainty. This is our hope. **In Christ, we are new. In Christ, we are free. In Christ, we are forever loved.**

CHAPTER 22
Taking Care of Yourself

The healing was a turning point, a transition from a period of pain and bewilderment to a new beginning. But healing, whether physical, emotional, or spiritual, **is not a point of arrival, but a point of departure.**

After my deliverance, after God had touched my heart and restored my life, I had a new reality before me: **Now I could truly live.**

I was no longer oppressed, I was no longer a slave to the past, I was no longer a prisoner of my fears. But I knew well that, once we are freed, we must learn to **guard the freedom** that God has given us.

Spiritual Vigilance: Not Falling Back into Slavery

The Bible warns us in very clear words:

"When the unclean spirit goes out of a man, it wanders about in dry places, seeking rest; and, finding none, he says: 'I will return to my house from which I came out'. And when he gets there, he finds it swept and adorned. Then he goes and takes with him seven other spirits worse than himself, and they enter and inhabit it; and that man's last condition becomes worse than the first." *(Luke 11:24-26)*

What does this mean?

It means that after we have received healing and deliverance, **we must guard our hearts, protect our faith, and stand firm in the Lord**.

Many, after a period of great grace, let their guard down. They feel safe, they think that nothing can touch them anymore, and so slowly they stop praying, they stop attending the community, they stop nourishing their souls with the Word of God.

And at that moment, the enemy returns.

Not because he has more power than before, but because he finds his heart **empty**.

A heart that is no longer inhabited by the presence of God is a vulnerable heart. It is like a house that, although it has been cleaned, has not been filled with a new life.

We must learn to **fill our hearts with God's presence**, so that no other influence can take over.

The Journey of Faith: A Constant Relationship with God

So, after my recovery, I started a new lifestyle:

- **I went to Mass every day.**

- **I went to confession frequently, to keep my heart pure.**

- **I studied God's Word every day, to know His will.**

- **I prayed constantly, establishing a true relationship with Jesus, as between two friends.**

It was not an obligation, it was not an empty religious routine. It was the desire to **remain steadfast in Christ**, to grow in my faith, to deepen my relationship with Him.

I had finally understood that **faith is not an isolated event, but a continuous journey**.

My spiritual life was to become **a healthy dependence on God**.

The Holy Spirit: Guide and Protection

One of the most wonderful aspects of my new life was the tangible presence of the **Holy Spirit**.

I had always heard of the Holy Spirit, but it wasn't until after I got my recovery that I experienced how real it was, how alive it was, how close it was to us.

"I will pray the Father, and He will give you another Comforter, to be with you forever: the Spirit of truth." *(John 14:16-17)*

The Holy Spirit is not an abstract idea, it is not a mere inspiration. **He is a person, the third person of the Trinity, and he is the One who guides us, protects us, strengthens us.**

When we walk in the Spirit:

- **He shows us the way to follow.**

- **He protects us from physical and spiritual dangers.**

- **He gives us his gifts for our own good and for the good of others.**

- **He comforts us in times of pain and difficulty.**

The Holy Spirit is the true **Comforter**. Just as a loving parent calms the crying of a child, so the Holy Spirit can calm **our fears, our anxieties, our anxieties.**

Thanksgiving Prayer: A New Attitude of Life

Another valuable lesson I learned during that time was **the importance of thanksgiving**.

We are often accustomed to **praying to ask**:

- "Lord, help me."

- "Lord, deliver me."

- "Lord, heal me."

And of course, God listens to us and answers us. But what do we do **after** we have received it?

Do we know how **to thank God**?

"In everything give thanks, for this is the will of God in Christ Jesus for you." *(1 Thessalonians 5:18)*

Thanking God changes our hearts.

When we learn to give thanks:

- **We begin to see blessings even in small things.**

- **Our hearts are filled with peace and trust.**

- **We are reminded every day that God is faithful.**

So I started **writing down the things I was grateful for every day**.

I wrote about the small everyday things, the big victories, the moments of grace. And the more I wrote, the more I realized how much God had been present in my life.

If we stop to reflect, we will see that **there are infinite mercies that enrich us every day**.

And not only in the past: **God continues to bless us, even today, even now.**

True Peace: Only in Christ

After a year of struggles, suffering, healing, I finally found **deep peace**.

It was not the peace of the world, which depends on circumstances.

It was the peace that only Christ can give.

"I leave you peace; My peace I give to you. I do not give you as the world gives. Let not your hearts be troubled, and do not be afraid." *(John 14:27)*

This peace is not found in anyone else. It is not found in success, it is not found in people, it is not found in material possessions.

It is found only in the Lord.

For two years, after my recovery, I walked with this awareness.

It was as if I were doing **spiritual physiotherapy**: every day I was nourished by the Word, by prayer, by the presence of God.

And so my faith was strengthened, my heart remained steadfast, my life was filled with light.

Conclusion: Guarding the Grace Received

Healing is not a point of arrival, but a new beginning.

If God has set us free, we must guard our freedom. If God has healed us, we must protect our healing. If God has touched us, we must stay close to Him.

We cannot go back. We cannot let our guard down. We cannot allow the enemy to regain control.

We must **walk with God every day**, living in prayer, in the Word, in gratitude.

And so, day after day, our life will be a continuous crescendo of grace, peace and love.

Because **he who abides in Christ never wavers**.

CHAPTER 23

Extraordinary Minister of the Eucharist

The first great work that God accomplished in my life after my spiritual "resurrection" was the gift of being able to become **an Extraordinary Minister of the Eucharist**.

It was a privilege I never imagined, a gift I could not deserve, yet God in his infinite mercy called me to serve in a new, deeper, more intimate way.

The Eucharist, the Sacrament of Love, had always been at the center of my faith, but now **it became part of my mission**.

The Eucharist: The Heart of the Christian Faith

The Eucharist is not a symbol, it is not a simple rite, **it is the very heart of Christian life**.

St. John Paul II said:

"The Eucharist is the greatest gift that the Church has received from her Lord, because it is the gift of himself, of his Person in his holy humanity and of his work of salvation." *(Ecclesia de Eucharistia, 11)*

Jesus, on the night before his Passion, left his disciples **a testament of love**.

"This is my body, which is given for you; Do this in remembrance of me. This cup is the new covenant in my blood, which is poured out for you." *(Luke 22:19-20)*

In those words there was everything:

- **The total offering of himself for the salvation of humanity.**

- **The invitation to nourish ourselves with his Body and Blood in order to have eternal life.**

- **The promise of his living and real presence in our midst.**

And yet, how many times do we attend Mass without realizing the immense gift we receive?

How often do we approach the Eucharist with distraction, without due respect, without true adoration?

Jesus is there, **alive**, before us.

It is not a piece of bread. **He is the living God, who gives himself completely for us.**

The Extraordinary Minister of the Eucharist: A Service of Love

The Church, in her wisdom, has instituted the *Extraordinary Minister of Communion* to allow the faithful to receive the Body of Christ even in particular situations.

In the Instruction *Immensae Caritatis* of January 29, 1973, the Church recognized that:

"Such a great mystery must be ever more deeply known and lived with intensity. The Extraordinary Minister is called to serve this mystery, fostering piety towards the Eucharist and helping the Christian community to participate fully in the grace of this sacrament."

Being an Extraordinary Minister of the Eucharist is not just **an assignment**, it is **a call**.

Signifies:

- **To be instruments of God to bring His Body to the faithful.**

- **Approach the Sacrament with fear and reverence.**

- **Serve with humility, knowing that the true Protagonist is Christ.**

- **To be witnesses of Jesus' love for humanity.**

When I was called to this ministry, I understood that God was asking me to **give myself even more**.

It was not enough to have received healing. It was not enough to have returned to life. Now was the time to **serve**, to put my life at the service of the Gospel.

Why take the Eucharist often?

The Eucharist is **the only permanent Sacrament,** that is, **the only one that we can receive several times during our Christian life**.

But why is it so important to take it often?

1. Because it is the Sacrament of Unity with Christ

Every time we receive the Eucharist, **we become one with Jesus**.

"He who eats my flesh and drinks my blood abides in me, and I in him." *(John 6:56)*

It is not just a symbolic act. Jesus **enters** us, lives in us, transforms us from within.

2. Because it purifies and strengthens us

When we approach the Eucharist **with a pure heart**, it becomes a **source of grace and spiritual strength**.

"He that eateth this bread shall live forever." *(John 6:58)*

But be careful: **we cannot receive the Eucharist in a state of mortal sin**.

St. Paul warns us:

"Whoever eats the bread or drinks the cup of the Lord unworthily will be guilty of the body and blood of the Lord." *(1 Corinthians 11:27)*

For this reason, **frequent confession is essential**.

3. Because it transforms us into Christ

The Eucharist is not only **a gift to be received**, but **a call to become what we receive**.

St. Augustine said:

"If you are the Body of Christ and its members, your mystery is placed on the table of the Lord: receive your mystery."

It means that, as we approach the Eucharist, **we must become more and more like Christ**.

- **More patients.**

- **More humble.**

- **More merciful.**

- **More willing to give our lives for others.**

Christ's Sacrifice: A Crucified Love

The Eucharist **is the sacrifice of Christ**.

It is not a new crucifixion, but **the actualization** of the one redeeming sacrifice of Jesus on the Cross.

Every time we participate in Mass, we are **under the Cross**, together with Mary, John, the disciples.

Yet, how many times do we forget it?

How many times are we distracted, tired, in a hurry?

Jesus is waiting for us at the altar. And us? **Do we know how to respond with love?**

Conclusion: The Eucharist, Source of Life

Becoming an Extraordinary Minister of the Eucharist **was an immense grace for me**.

He taught me:

- **To serve with humility.**

- **To live every Mass with an adoring heart.**

- **To recognize the living presence of Jesus in the Sacrament.**

- **To nourish myself often with the Eucharist to receive strength and light.**

The Eucharist **is not a prize for the perfect, but a nourishment for pilgrims**, for those who walk in faith, among the joys and hardships of life.

If we want to remain steadfast, if we want to grow, **we cannot do without this Bread of Life**.

Let us approach it with faith, with love, with gratitude.

And every time we receive the Holy Host, let us remember:

Jesus is here. Jesus is alive. Jesus is for us.

And in the silence of our hearts, let his voice resound:

"He who comes to me will hunger no more, and he who believes in me will never thirst." *(John 6:35)*

Chapter 24
Do I have a "Special" Vocation?

Every day that the Lord allows us to live is a gift. Not a coincidence, not a succession of meaningless events, but an opportunity **conceived, desired, prepared for us** from eternity.

If God created us, if he calls us by name and knows us deeply, then he is also the One who knows **what can really make us happy**.

Yet, many of us spend much of our lives **searching for direction**, asking ourselves:

- Why am I here?

- What should I do with my life?

- Do I really have a vocation?

- What is the path that God has planned for me?

These questions are fundamental, because they push us to reflect on the **meaning of our existence**.

Vocation is not an abstract idea, nor something that concerns only priests or consecrated persons. **We all have a vocation.** We are all called to **carry out the plan of love that God has planned for us.**

But how can we recognize it? How can we discern the voice of God in the midst of the many voices of the world and of our hearts?

Vocation: A Response to God

Vocation is the answer to what God has planned for us. It is not we who choose our call, **it is God who calls us** and reveals to us, step by step, his plan for us.

Our part is **to listen, understand and respond.** And it is precisely here that the big question opens: **will we say "Yes" or will we say "No"?**

To recognize our vocation it is necessary:

1. **Cultivating an authentic relationship with God**

    - Pray, read His Word, participate in the sacraments.

    - Without constant dialogue with the Lord, it is impossible to discern his will.

2. **Be Alert to Signs**

    - God does not speak in a magical or spectacular way, but through the signs of life.

    - The situations we live, the people we meet, the passions that animate us, the experiences that touch us are **instruments through which God speaks to us**.

3. **Have the courage to question yourself**

- Vocation is never a simple "doing", but becoming.

- God does not call us only to a task, but to be **who we really are**.

- This requires looking within ourselves with sincerity and asking: *Am I really following the right path?*

4. **Discerning with patience and trust**

    - Discernment is not an immediate process.

    - It takes **time, prayer, inner listening** and **dialogue with those who can help us** (spiritual directors, guides, people of faith).

God gives us everything we need to respond

God never calls a person **without equipping him or her** with what is needed to answer his call.

If he has a plan for us, he also gives us the **talents, charisms, abilities and graces necessary** to carry it out.

Here's why it's important **to know yourself**:

- **What are my gifts?**

- **What am I passionate about?**

- **In what do I feel I can give the best of me?**

- **What are the things that make me feel most fulfilled?**

The vocation is already **written within us**, but we are often distracted, afraid or unable to read it. Sometimes we go around in circles for years because **we don't take the time to listen to God** and understand **what really belongs to us**.

But God is **the first to believe in us, the first to bet on us**, and for this reason he gives us all the graces we need to respond with generosity.

The freedom to choose

God never forces anyone. He calls us, shows us the way, gives us signs... **But the choice is ours.**

Responding to a vocation means **giving oneself totally to God**, with freedom and love. It is not a prison, but a **path of fulfillment and fullness**.

This is why discernment is **an art that is learned**:

- **You grow in knowing how to listen.**

- **You learn to recognize true desires from transient ones.**

- **One acquires the ability to read the events of life in the light of faith.**

It is in calm, silence, and prayer that we can **hear the gentle breeze of God's voice** (1 Kings 19:12).

Vocation and meaning of life

Many people today are experiencing **a crisis of meaning**.

Psychiatrist Viktor Frankl said:

"Today's forms of neurosis, in many cases, can be traced back to existential frustration, to a failure to realize the human aspiration towards an existence that is as meaningful as possible."

In other words, **if we do not discover the meaning of our existence, we feel lost, frustrated, unhappy.**

Our vocation is **what gives meaning to our lives**.

When we find **what we were created for**, everything changes:

- **Difficulties become tests to be faced with confidence.**

- **Joys multiply because they are lived in gratitude.**

- **The heart is filled with peace because we know we are in the right place.**

Discovering one's vocation does not mean **avoiding the hardships of life**, but it means **having a clear direction, a certain hope, a deep joy that no storm can extinguish**.

Conclusion: Are You Willing To Say Your "Yes"?

Your vocation is already within you.

God created you with a **precise purpose**, with **a unique mission** that only you can fulfill.

The question is, **are you willing to listen? Are you willing to say your "I do"?**

Every call from God is **an act of love**.

Fear not. **If God calls you, it is because he has already prepared the way for you.**

And, whatever your vocation, remember:

There is no greater joy than that of living for the Lord, on the path that He has prepared for you.

The healing was a turning point, a transition from a period of pain and bewilderment to a new beginning. But healing, whether physical, emotional, or spiritual

CHAPTER 25
A Course with Obstacles? Yes

In the heart of every man and woman there is a deep desire to understand the meaning of their lives. We were not created to wander without direction, nor to live a meaningless existence. God has a dream for each of us.

But the road to find out is not always easy.

Sooner or later, we are all faced with moments of uncertainty, deep questions, doubts that seem to block us. **What should I do with my life? Am I really following God's will?**

These questions are precious, because they urge us to seek the truth more ardently. Pope Francis reminds us that:

"Each of us has a mission to fulfill"

We are not here by chance. Our life has a task, a meaning. **The problem is that we often don't see it right away.**

Questions and doubts: signs of an authentic journey

When you feel a deeper call in your heart, questions begin to arise that can shake you:

- **Lord, are you really calling me?**

- **Why do I feel incomplete, as if something is missing?**

- **Where do you want to take me, Holy Spirit?**

The discovery of one's vocation is not an instantaneous enlightenment, but a path that requires **time, discernment, prayer and silence**.

God does not impose himself by force, but leaves us the freedom to seek him.

The problem is that **we live in a noisy, distracted, confused world**, where finding moments of quiet to listen to God is increasingly difficult.

How much space do we leave to God in our days?

If we really want to understand His plan for us, we must learn **to stop, to be silent, to recognize the signs that He sends us.**

The fears that stand in the way

Discovering one's vocation is not just a matter of desire or understanding. There are **concrete obstacles** that we have to face, the first of which is **fear**.

1. The fear of the unknown

What awaits me in the future? If I respond to God's call, what will change in my life? If I choose this path, will I really be happy?

The unknown scares us because it forces us **to get out of our comfort zone**. But every great call from God has always required an act of trust.

Think of Abraham, who left his land without knowing where God would take him. Think of Peter, who got out of the boat to walk on the water.

God does not reveal everything to us right away, because he wants us **to learn to trust him, step by step**.

2. The fear of failure

What if I take the wrong path? What if I made a choice that turned out to be wrong? Can we go back?

This is one of the greatest fears: **the fear of not being good enough, of disappointing God, of making a decision and then regretting it.**

But God doesn't ask us to be perfect. He only asks us **to entrust ourselves to Him**, to do our best and not to fear mistakes.

Even if we make a mistake, God will be able to straighten our way. He never leaves us alone.

The Distractions of the World: A Silent Enemy

In addition to inner fears, there is another obstacle that often distances us from God: **the distractions of the world.**

We live in an age in which **everything distracts us**, everything takes us away from ourselves:

- TV, social media, newspapers, fashions, the opinions of others.

- The hectic commitments, the work, the thousand things to do.

- The need to appear, to be accepted, to "be someone" in the eyes of the world.

All this creates **noise** inside us.

How can we listen to God's voice **if our hearts are always filled with thoughts and worries?**

Learning to be silent

If we really want to find our way, we must **learn to carve out spaces of silence**, moments in which we can stop and listen to God.

- **Turn off your phone for a while.**

- **Detach yourself from social media and the opinions of the world.**

- **Carve out moments of prayer and reflection.**

- **Spend time reading God's Word.**

Only in silence can we recognize **the signs that God sends us** and understand what our true path is.

Discernment: Choosing wisely

Discerning one's vocation is not easy. It takes time, patience and trust.

How can we tell if God is really calling us?

Here are some basic steps in discernment:

1. **Constant prayer** – Ask God to enlighten our hearts.

2. **Inner listening** – What deep desires do we feel within ourselves?

3. **Observing signs** – God speaks to us through life's situations.

4. **Confrontation with people of faith** – A spiritual father, a priest, a guide can help us see more clearly.

5. **The courage to trust** – You can't wait until you have all the answers before taking the first step.

God does not expect us to be perfect, but that we are **willing to follow him with love and trust.**

Conclusion: A path worth walking

Yes, the path of life is full of obstacles. Yes, there will be moments of doubt, fear, uncertainty. But **it's worth it**.

Because, when we discover the path that God has prepared for us, everything makes sense. Challenges become trials to be faced with faith. Questions are answered in trust in God. Fear gives way to the joy of discovery.

If you feel that God is calling you, don't be afraid. Open your heart, listen, and **let Him guide you.**

You're not alone. God is with you, and he walks by your side.

And **whatever your vocation**, always remember:

"Do not be afraid! Open, indeed, open wide the doors to Christ!" (St. John Paul II)

CHAPTER 26
Discernment in Silence

One of the foundations of the Christian life is that God **never stops speaking** to his people. He addresses each one of us with love, patience, and care, eager to establish a personal and authentic relationship.

The problem is not that God does not speak to us. **The problem is that we don't know how to listen to him.**

We live in a world full of noise. Our days are hectic, filled with commitments, worries, thoughts, a thousand distractions. We are constantly bombarded with sounds, words, images, news, opinions and opinions.

And in this chaos, **where does the voice of God find its place?**

God does not impose himself, he does not shout to be heard. God speaks in **silence**, with a subtle and delicate voice, which can only be grasped if we are willing to stop and listen.

But silence is frightening.

Today man flees silence because he fears being alone with himself. He is afraid of what he might discover within himself. He is afraid to face the deepest questions. And so he fills every moment of his life with distractions that keep him away from himself and from God.

But if we want to discern the Lord's will for our lives, if we want to understand His plan for us, **we must learn the art of silence.**

The importance of silence in the spiritual journey

Silence is the space in which God reveals himself

When we read the Bible, we find that **God often manifests himself in silence.**

- The prophet Elijah, on Mount Horeb, **does not find God in the rushing wind, earthquake or fire,** but in **a gentle breeze** (1 Kings 19:11-13).

- Jesus himself, before the great decisions and in the most crucial moments of his mission, withdrew **in solitude and prayer** to listen to the voice of the Father.

Silence is not just the absence of noise. Silence is a **sacred space** in which we can listen to God.

Silence allows us to listen to our heart

We cannot discern our vocation if we do not learn to listen to ourselves.

But our hearts are often suffocated by a thousand inner voices:

- Daily worries.

- The wounds of the past.

- Fears for the future.

- The expectations of others.

- Doubts and insecurities.

All these thoughts **create a deafening noise within us**, which prevents us from recognizing God's voice.

If we want to clarify, **we must learn to be silent within ourselves.**

How to cultivate silence?

Silence is not something that can be improvised. It is an art that is learned and cultivated.
Here are some concrete steps to rediscover its value:

1. Create spaces of silence throughout the day

If we really want to give space to God, we must learn to **carve out moments of silence** every day.

- **In the morning**, before starting the day, take at least 10 minutes of silence and prayer.

- **During the day**, try to stop for a moment, close your eyes, breathe, make room for God.

- **In the evening**, turn off your cell phone and TV for a few minutes, and reflect on your day before the Lord.

God speaks in the moments when we stop. If we are always running, we will never be able to feel it.

2. Learn to turn off distractions

We live in a world that keeps us connected all the time: notifications, social media, messages, videos, news.

But if we want to rediscover silence, we must **learn to disconnect** for a while.

- Reduce the time you spend on social media.

- Avoid filling every free moment with your phone or TV.

- Learn to be **alone with yourself**, without the need for external stimuli.

Silence is a school of **inner freedom**. The more we learn to extinguish the superfluous, the more we leave room for God.

3. The prayer of the heart: transforming silence into dialogue with God

Silence is not empty. Silence is **the space in which God speaks to us**.

We can fill it with the **prayer of the heart**, a simple, spontaneous prayer that is born within us:

- **An act of trust**: "Lord, here I am. Speak, your servant hears you."

- **A thanksgiving**: "Thank you, Jesus, for this day."

- **An invocation**: "Holy Spirit, guide me".

Even just **repeating Jesus' name in silence** can help us to commune with Him.

The fruits of silence: what changes in our lives?

When we learn to cultivate silence, wonderful things happen:

1. **We find inner peace** Silence calms the mind and heart. It helps us to live with more serenity, without anxieties and worries.

2. **We discover who we really are** In silence we learn to listen to ourselves, to understand our deepest desires, to recognize our vocation.

3. **Developing a more authentic relationship with God** Prayer is no longer just words recited in haste, but becomes **a true dialogue** with the Lord.

4. **We improve our relationship with others**
   When we learn to listen to ourselves and God, we also learn **to listen to others** with more love and attention.

Conclusion: Silence, a way to God

Silence is not empty. Silence is **the door to enter into the presence of God**.

Today more than ever, we need to rediscover it. We need to stop, to turn off the external and internal noise, and **to listen.**

God is there, always ready to speak to us.

The question is: **are we willing to listen to him?**

If you truly want to discern God's plan for your life, **start with silence**. And there, deep in your heart, you will find His voice guiding you.

Chapter 27
The Choice of the OFS Vocation

Among the many paths that God offers to His children to follow Him and love Him, there is a **particular and precious** way, that of the **vocation to the Secular Franciscan Order (OFS).**

This call, which has its roots in the experience of **St. Francis of Assisi**, is a concrete and profound way to live the Gospel **in daily life**, as lay people, without taking religious vows, but with an equally radical commitment.

Those who choose to enter the OFS do not leave the world to retire to a convent, but choose **to sanctify the world from within**, bringing the light of Christ **into families, professions, and society**.

The Secular Franciscan Order is **a journey of life**, a school of spirituality and a way to be authentic witnesses of the Kingdom of God, right where one is.

But what does it really mean **to embrace the secular Franciscan vocation**? What are the fundamental aspects of this choice? And how can the example of St. Francis be concretely lived in the world?

The Heart of the Secular Franciscan Vocation

Those who feel in their hearts the call to follow St. Francis in the world, discover a precious treasure, a path of holiness that is nourished by **poverty, humility, joy and fraternity**.

Franciscan spirituality is not made up of **great theories**, but of **simple and concrete gestures**, which transform life and make it **a living witness to the Gospel**.

The Secular Franciscan does not seek **greatness in the eyes of the world**, but allows himself to be **shaped by the Lord**, to be an **instrument of peace and love**, like Francis of Assisi.

Here are the five fundamental characteristics of the OFS vocation:

1. Franciscan Spirituality: Living the Gospel with Joy and Simplicity

To be a Franciscan means **to embrace the spirit of the Gospel wholeheartedly**. It means living with **simplicity, joy and interior poverty**, trusting completely in Providence.

St. Francis did not seek wealth or power, but found **joy in simple things**:

- in **the smile of a brother**,

- in **the beauty of creation**,

- in **silent prayer**,

- in **the service of the least**.

Those who choose the Franciscan way commit themselves to **freeing themselves from the superfluous**, to be lighter on the journey of life and more open to the voice of God.

2. The Commitment to Communion: Fraternity as a Way of Life

No Franciscan is **alone**.

St. Francis founded an order **of brothers and sisters**, because he understood that Christian life is a **community journey**.

Being a secular Franciscan means **living fraternity as a gift and commitment**:

- it means **walking together**, supporting each other in difficult moments,

- it means **praying for one another**,

- it means **sharing faith and love for God**.

The OFS fraternities are true spiritual **families**, where we grow together **in faith, charity and mission**.

3. Witness in Everyday Life: The Gospel in Everyday Life

Being a Christian does not mean **living the faith only on Sundays**, but bringing Jesus **into every area of our lives**.

The Secular Franciscan is called to **be a witness to the Gospel**:

- **in the family**, living love and forgiveness,

- **in work**, bringing honesty and justice,

- **in society**, committing himself to peace and solidarity.

Francis said: **"Preach the Gospel, and if necessary, also use words."**

The Secular Franciscan **does not only speak of God, but shows it with his life**.

4. Continuing Formation: Growing in Faith and Service

The Franciscan vocation is not a point of arrival, but **a path of continuous growth**.

Those who enter the OFS commit themselves to **formation**, to study the Word of God, the life of St. Francis, the doctrine of the Church, to become mature **and aware** disciples.

Formation is not only **theoretical**, but must be translated into **concrete action**, into an authentic evangelical lifestyle.

5. Service to Others: Love with Concrete Gestures

Faith without works is **dead**.

Those who choose the Franciscan way put themselves at the **service of others**, especially the least and the suffering.

St. Francis teaches us that **seeing Christ in the face of the poor** is the way to truly encounter God.

The Secular Franciscan is therefore committed to **serving**, to **giving his time and heart**, to **bringing hope and comfort to those in need**.

A Path of Holiness in the World

Being a secular Franciscan is a call **to holiness**, lived **in everyday life**.

It is not a question of doing extraordinary things, but of **living ordinary things in an extraordinary way**.

Being a Franciscan means **looking at life with different eyes**, with the certainty that **every moment is a gift from God** and that everything can be lived with a spirit of **gratitude, trust and love**.

St. Francis said:

"Start by doing what is necessary, then what is possible, and suddenly you will find yourself doing the impossible."

Those who choose the OFS vocation choose **to let themselves be transformed by God's love**, to be a **light in the world**, a **bridge of peace**, a **witness to the joy of the Gospel**.

Conclusion: The Beauty of the Secular Franciscan Vocation

The OFS vocation is **a gift and a responsibility**.

It is a **deep and joyful journey of faith**, a way to sanctify the world with the **power of simplicity and love**.

Those who hear this call **must not be afraid**, but open their hearts and trust in God.

St. Francis was not a special man **in himself**, but he became one because he said **yes** to the Lord with all his heart.

And if God has done great things with him, he can also do them with us.

Because **every vocation is a dream of God that is fulfilled in our lives.**

If you feel that this path belongs to you, do not hesitate.

Entrust yourself to the Lord, enter the Fraternity and let yourself be transformed by His love.

The world needs real witnesses. The world needs **Secular Franciscans**.

CHAPTER 28

Consecrated Life, the Way

Consecrated life is an **extraordinary gift** that God has given to His Church through the Holy Spirit. It is a **profound and radical call**, a total yes to God that transforms the entire existence of those who welcome him.

When a man or woman chooses the path of consecration, they are not only making a personal decision, but responding **to a dream of God**, accepting to become **a visible sign of His love in the world**.

This vocation is not an escape from the world, but an **immersion even more deeply in reality**, with our gaze fixed on Christ. It is a powerful witness, a life that cries out **with the power of silence**, prayer and service.

In the Gospel, Jesus himself lived virginity, poverty and obedience, three signs that characterize every consecrated person:

- **Virginity**, because the heart of the consecrated person is entirely of God and of others, without divisions, loving with pure and universal love.

- **Poverty**, because the consecrated person strips himself of himself in order to entrust himself entirely to Providence, without possessing anything but having everything.

- **Obedience**, because one no longer follows one's own will, but that of God, with absolute trust.

Those who live this call become **a visible sign of Christ's presence in the world**.

A Vision of Life: Looking Beyond the Ephemeral

Consecrated life is like **a window open to eternity**. Those who choose this path **see what really matters**, grasp the **gift of life** with open arms and do not let themselves be chained by ephemeral desires.

St. Francis of Assisi, speaking of his conversion, said:

"What before seemed bitter to me, changed into sweetness of soul and body."

Even today, in a world that runs towards **emptiness**, consecrated life is a beacon.

We live in a time when **the meaning of life is being lost**, where young people seem **hopeless, rootless and ideal**. Many take refuge in fun, in the artificial paradises of technology and social media, in momentary illusions, trying to anesthetize their hearts.

Yet, **the human heart needs God**.

Today's culture proposes models that push us to search for the ephemeral, to individualism, to superficiality. But the consecrated person is **a voice that cries out in the desert**, he is someone who with his life reminds us that there is **something greater**, deeper, eternal.

Consecration is **a radical alternative**, a revolution of love, a choice that goes against the tide.

The Consecrated Person: Witness of a New Hope

To be consecrated today means **to be a sign of hope in a world without hope**.

St. John Paul II said:

"Consecrated life is a precious and necessary gift for the present and future of the people of God."

But how can a consecrated person **be hope for the world?**

1. With the Testimony of a Happy and Full Life

The world needs **authentic witnesses**, not sad and inward-looking people. A consecrated person is not a man or woman who renounces happiness, but **someone who has discovered true joy**.

A life lived in communion with God is **a fulfilled life**. A consecrated person who lives with enthusiasm, serenity, and fullness, becomes **attractive**, raises questions, gives rise to desires for the infinite.

Many young people turn away from the faith because they do not see Christians **who are joyful and full of life**. And yet, holiness is the way of the truest joy.

The consecrated person must not be **a sad shadow in the world**, but **a shining light**, a reflection of God's beauty.

2. With Love for the Last

A true consecrated person **does not close in on himself**, but goes out, goes out to meet others, takes care of the weakest. Love for the poor, for the marginalized, for the suffering is **a fundamental characteristic of consecrated life**.

Mother Teresa of Calcutta said:

"Not all of us can do great things, but we can do small things with great love."

The world needs **hands that serve, hearts that love, eyes that see pain and welcome it.**

3. With a Deep Prayer Life

A consecrated person is first and foremost **a man or woman of prayer.**

In silence, in adoration, in meditation on the Word of God, the consecrated person finds **his strength, his peace, his mission.**

We live in a hectic time, where **everyone runs and no one stops.**

But those who know how to stop **in prayer**, those who know how to find time for God, become a prophetic sign.

The consecrated person is not only **someone who prays**, but **someone who lives in constant union with God.** His life becomes **incarnate prayer**, a continuous dialogue with the Father.

Consecrated Life: An Appeal to the Church Today

Today more than ever, the Church needs **new vocations to the consecrated life**.

Not because there is a lack of people, but because **the world needs visible signs of God's love**.

Consecrated life is not **a reality of the past**, but an **ever-present call**.

Those who consecrate themselves to God do not choose a sterile life, but **a fruitful life**, which bears fruit **in the Church and in the world**.

The consecrated vocation must **shine,** it must be a **visible and credible sign**.

Because it is **the beauty of consecrated life that attracts**, not words or theories.

Conclusion: Don't Be Afraid to Say Yes

If you feel a call in your heart, **don't ignore it**.

Do not be afraid to leave everything for God. Do not be afraid to **live a total, radical, unreserved love**.

St. Francis left everything to follow Christ, and his life **illuminated the world**. St. Clare did the same, and her example **continues to transform lives**.

Consecrated life **is not a loss, but an infinite gain**.

As Jesus said:

"*Whoever loses his life for my sake will find it*" (Mt 16:25).

Those who consecrate themselves to God lose nothing, but find **the greatest joy**: to live **in the very heart of God** and to bring His love into the world.

If you feel the Lord calling you, **listen to His voice**.

Respond boldly.

And you will discover that there is **nothing more beautiful than** belonging entirely to Him.

CHAPTER 29
Charisms, Gifts of the Holy Spirit

At the heart of the Christian life there is an extraordinary secret: **God does not leave us alone, but fills us with His gifts**. These special gifts, called **charisms**, are much more than simple human talents or capacities: they are supernatural gifts, gifts of grace, which the Holy Spirit distributes **to each one as he** wishes, so that every Christian can be a light in the world.

Saint Paul, in his First Letter to the Corinthians, reminds us that **charisms are not a personal privilege, but a service for the good of all**:

"There are diversities of charisms, but the Spirit is one; there are diversities of ministries, but the Lord is one; there are diversities of operations, but there is only one God, who works all things in all. To each one is given a particular manifestation of the Spirit for the common good." (1 Cor 12:4-7)

Here, then, is the fundamental principle: **charisms are not for us, but for others**. They are not given to exalt a person's ego, but to **build up**

community and to make God's love visible in the world.

What are the Charisms?

The Holy Spirit **distributes His gifts according to His will**. Each believer can receive one or more of them, but always for **the purpose of serving and glorifying God**.

St. Paul lists some fundamental charisms:

- **The gift of wisdom**, to understand divine truths with a special light.

- **The gift of knowledge**, to discern the truth and mystery of creation.

- **The gift of faith**, an unshakable trust in the power of God.

- **The gift of healing**, to be an instrument of physical and spiritual healing.

- **The gift of miracles**, extraordinary signs of divine intervention.

- **The gift of prophecy**, to communicate God's will.

- **The gift of discernment of spirits**, to recognize what comes from God and what is deception.

- **The gift of tongues**, to speak in unknown tongues in the context of prayer.

- **The gift of interpreting tongues**, to translate and make understandable what is said in the Spirit.

These gifts are not mere "powers," but **instruments by which God works in the world through us**. But there is one gift that is superior to all others: **love**.

The Greatest Charism: Love

Saint Paul warns us: we can have **all the charisms**, we can be powerful in faith, we can even perform miracles... but if **we don't have love, we are nothing**.

"Even if I speak in the tongues of men and angels, but do not have love, I am like a sounding brass or a tinkling cymbal. And if I had the gift of prophecy and knew all the mysteries and all the knowledge, and possessed the fullness of faith so as to move mountains, but did not have charity, I am nothing." (1 Cor 13:1-2)

Love is **the heart of all charisms**. Without it, even the most extraordinary gifts become useless.

Authentic love is not a passing emotion, but a daily choice. Saint Paul describes it in wonderful words:

- **Charity is patient**

- **Charity Is Kind**

- **She is not envious**

- **He doesn't brag**

- **It does not swell with pride**

- **Not disrespectful**

- **It does not seek its own interest**

- **He does not get angry**

- **It does not take into account the evil received**

- **He does not rejoice in injustice, but delights in the truth**

- **He covers everything, believes everything, hopes everything, endures everything**

True love is not a superficial feeling, but **a force that transforms**, that breaks down walls, that conquers evil with good. For this reason, **without love, even the most powerful of charisms is vain**.

The Risk of Spiritual Pride

Charisms are wonderful gifts, but they can also become **a temptation**. Those who receive them can fall into the mistake of believing that they are **a sign of superiority** over others.

Jesus Himself warned His disciples:

"Many will say to me in that day, Lord, Lord, have we not prophesied in your name? And in your name have we not cast out demons? And in your name have we not performed many wonders? But then I will declare to them: I have never known you. Depart from me, you workers of iniquity!" (Mt 7:22-23)

This teaches us that **it is not enough to have charisms to be pleasing to God**. What matters is **humility and service**, because everything we have is a gift.

If a charism leads **to putting oneself at the center**, to seeking applause or recognition, it means that it has been distorted. True charisms do not inflate the ego, but **lead to serving with love and discretion**.

How to Recognize and Develop Your Charisms?

Many people ask themselves: **"What is my charisma? How can I find out?"**

Five steps to discern charisms

1. **Pray sincerely** Ask the Holy Ghost to reveal to you what gifts He has prepared for you. God does not give charisms at random, but according to your mission in the world.

2. **Observing the Fruits** What actions bring joy and peace to your heart? In what areas do you feel an inner strength that does not come from you?

3. **Listening to the community** Often it is others who recognize our charisms before us. Ask your

brothers and sisters in faith what gifts they see in you.

4. **Being willing to serve** Charisms do not emerge in a vacuum, but in service. Offer to help in the community, and you will discover what gifts God has placed in you.

5. **Maintain humility** Remember: **charisms are for edifying others, not for our ego**. The more humble you remain, the more the Spirit can work in you.

Conclusion: One body, many members, one spirit

The Church is **a body with many members**, and each has a unique role. There are no "better" or "worse" gifts, for **all serve the building of the Kingdom**.

True greatness lies not in receiving the most spectacular charisms, but **in serving with love and fidelity**.

Remember Jesus' words:

"Whoever wants to be the greatest among you, let him be the servant of all." (Mt 20:26)

Charisms are **a call to service**. And the greatest of all is **love**.

If you live with love, then **you are already a sign of God's presence in the world**.

CHAPTER 30
Conclusions – The Victory of God's Love

Throughout our journey of faith, through the previous chapters, we have contemplated the beauty of consecrated life, the richness of charisms, the depth of vocation and the call to live the Gospel in everyday life. But now, having reached the end of this reflection, it is necessary to raise our gaze to the heart of the Christian message: **God's love is the supreme force that conquers all things**.

There is no obstacle that God's love cannot overcome. There is no sin that His mercy cannot forgive. There is no darkness that His light cannot dispel.

The **absolute culmination of this truth** is found in the **death and resurrection of Jesus Christ**. He faced pain, suffering and death, shouldering the weight of humanity's sin on his shoulders. It seemed like the ultimate defeat. Yet, precisely in the darkest moment of history, **love triumphed**.

Christ is risen! And with him, hope conquered despair, life defeated death, grace annihilated sin.

This is **the great victory of God's love**:

"Where, O death, is your victory? Where, O death, is your sting?" (1 Cor 15:55)

If there is one certainty that always accompanies us, it is this: God's **love will never fail**.

A Love That Transforms the World

God's love is not an abstract concept. It is not a philosophical idea or a passing feeling. God's love is **action**, it is **concreteness**, it is **power that transforms reality**.

Where there is hatred, His love brings peace. Where there is despair, His love brings hope. Where there is loneliness, His love brings communion. Where there is sin, His love brings forgiveness.

Jesus' sacrifice on the cross was not only an act of suffering, but an **act of absolute love**. Every wound, every humiliation, every drop of blood shed was the price of our redemption.

Yet, **love did not stop at the cross**. Three days later, **the stone of the tomb was rolled away** and Christ was risen.

This means that **there is no situation with no way out, there is no night that cannot be followed by dawn**.

That is why God's love is not just a personal experience, but **a mission to be brought to the world**. We are called to be witnesses of this victory!

The Believer, Witness of the Victory of Love

If God's love is the greatest force, then our task is clear: **to let it fill our lives and transform our hearts**.

We cannot remain spectators of this truth. We must make it our own, live it, proclaim it with our existence.

How can we witness the victory of God's love?

1. **Welcoming His Love** First of all, we must believe that God loves us. It may seem obvious, but often our hearts are closed, distrustful, unable to let themselves be loved to the end. God loves us **as we are**, with our frailties, our falls, our defects. We don't have to be perfect to be loved by Him. **We are loved and that's it.**

2. **Living in Love** Love is not something to be kept only for oneself. It is a gift that grows only if it is given. For this reason, we are called to live in charity, to serve our brothers and sisters, to forgive those who have hurt us, to build bridges instead of walls.

3. **Don't Be Afraid of the Cross** The cross is not the end, but the passage to the resurrection. There will be moments of pain in our lives, but **suffering does not have the last word**. If we rely on God, He will turn every tear into joy, every trial into an opportunity for growth.

4. **Proclaiming Hope** The world needs credible witnesses, men and women who know how to show, with their lives, that **God's love is real**. Every day we have the opportunity to bring hope to those around us, to spread light where there is darkness, to be instruments of the victory of God's love.

The New Life in Christ

To welcome the victory of God's love means **to be reborn to new life**. It is not just a matter of believing in an event from the past, but of **letting this truth change our existence, here and now**.

Every time we choose to love instead of hate, every time we choose to forgive instead of retaliate, every time we choose to serve instead of demand, **we are living Easter, we are witnessing Christ's victory over death**.

St. Paul reminds us:

> *"If anyone is in Christ, he is a new creation; old things have passed away, behold, new things have been born."* (2 Cor 5:17)

This is the beauty of our faith: **we are no longer prisoners of the past, we are no longer condemned by our mistakes**. In Christ, we are free. In Christ, we are new. In Christ, we are loved forever.

Conclusion: The Triumph of Love

We have spoken of vocation, of consecration, of charisms, of service. But **everything finds its meaning in a single truth**:

God loved us first, and His love conquered all.

This is the certainty that accompanies us every day. This is the hope that sustains us in difficulties. This is the promise that illuminates our future.

So, **let's not be afraid**. No matter what happens, we know that **love has already won**.

There is only one thing left for us to do: **to live this love, to bear witness to it, to proclaim it, and to let it transform the world through us.**

Because in the end, of all that exists, **only love will remain forever.**

"Now then these three things remain: faith, hope and charity. But the greatest of all is charity." (1 Cor 13:13)

Amen!

OTHER BOOKS LDN EDIZIONI

How to evangelize with Power: Learn how to talk about Jesus to people accompanied by the supernatural power of God

This is the time for the Church to enter into a new vision of evangelization, one with power. More than once we have been taught that the great commission that Jesus left us to go and preach the gospel (in Mark 16:15) is not just an invitation but an order. The Gospel of the kingdom of God must be preached in every corner of the world, and today more than ever there is an urgency for this message to reach every heart and transform every life supernaturally.

"How to Evangelize with Power" has been written with the purpose of teaching you to evangelize effectively through the power of the Holy Spirit accompanied by healings, deliverances, signs, miracles, and wonders. The Author's desire is that this book can help you to fulfil the greatest challenge that Jesus left us before he left and mobilize you to go down the streets and "Evangelize with Power."

Supernatural Experiences with God: Real Testimonies of a Supernatural God

"Supernatural Experiences with God" gathers real and engaging stories that carry important messages and meditations. Through this series of stories, the author shows what it means to listen to God's will, act by faith, and challenge the impossible. These principles and experiences are applicable in everyone's life and can help you whatever your situation.

PROPHETIC MANUAL: FOR TODAY'S AND TOMORROW'S PROPHETS

This manual is a culmination of insights gathered from our prophetic schools, tailored to provide a strong biblical foundation for those with the gift of prophecy and those called to speak for God. It shares valuable experiences and teachings to empower individuals in prophetic ministry, offering both guidance and practical application.

Through its pages, readers embark on a journey of discovery, growth, and empowerment, delving into biblical principles and prophetic insights. It aims to equip individuals with the tools needed to navigate the prophetic realm with confidence and clarity, inspiring them to embrace their calling with courage and conviction.

You will learn how to avoid common challenges and problems that may arise when prophesying and acquire the necessary tools to discern between a true prophet and a false one, as well as distinguish between genuine and false prophecies

Here, you will find a comprehensive guide to unleash the power of prophecy and how to apply it wisely in churches and everyday life. As you delve into these pages, you will receive an abundance of fundamental advice that will help you prophesy with wisdom and avoid common mistakes that often cause problems in church communities.

This book is an essential resource for those who wish to deepen their prophetic calling and aspire to serve as instruments of God on earth. Whether you consider yourself a prophet, possess the gift of prophecy, or simply desire a better understanding of this important ministry, this work will provide you with the necessary foundations, spiritual training, and practical guidance you need to thrive in the prophetic realm and fulfill your divine purpose.

Color the Bible: Animals and Bible Verses

"Color the Bible: Animals and Bible Verses" is an illustrated book that offers an exciting journey through the most beloved and significant stories of the Bible, specially adapted for children aged 4 to 8.

Is the perfect gift for young faith explorers. This exceptional Christian coloring book is designed for children aged 4 to 8 and offers a unique experience of learning and fun.

With 65 beautiful illustrations, this colouring book provides children with the opportunity to immerse themselves in the most famous Bible stories, enriching their understanding of the Bible while unleashing their creativity. Each illustration captures the magic of biblical stories and features fascinating scenes with animals, creating an engaging and educational experience.

The Fascinating Stories of the Bible

"The Fascinating Stories of the Bible" is an illustrated book that offers an exciting journey through the most beloved and significant stories of the Bible, specially adapted for children aged 4 to 8.

With clear and engaging language and vivid illustrations, this book makes the Bible accessible and captivating for young readers

This book is not just a retelling of Bible stories; it's an educational experience that teaches faith, morality, and compassion through powerful and timeless examples.

Perfect for home reading or for educational use in schools and religious communities, "The Fascinating Stories of the Bible" is a precious gift for every child, enriching their understanding of the world and its deeper values.

The Fascinating Stories of the Bible (Coloring Book)

"The Fascinating Stories of the Bible", a book that brings the extraordinary biblical tales directly to the hearts and minds of young readers through a creative and inspiring experience.

A Journey into Bible Stories: This book allows children aged 4 to 8 to immerse themselves in the most iconic stories of the Bible. Young readers can discover the message of faith while unleashing their creativity, coloring fascinating scenes, and reading relevant biblical verses.

Each page captures the magic of the biblical stories, creating an engaging and educational experience.

This book offers an educational and enjoyable experience, combining the creativity of coloring with learning biblical stories. Thanks to its inclusive approach, every child, regardless of their level of knowledge, will find interesting and understandable stimuli. Furthermore, it helps children develop a stronger bond with faith by engaging them spiritually.

How to Interpret Dreams

With the expert guidance of Apostle Vincenzo Petrarca, "How to Interpret Dreams" offers a revolutionary perspective on how dreams can serve as a bridge between us and God, providing profound insights into our lives and spiritual journeys.

This book is not only a manual for dream interpretation but also a transformative journey that integrates biblical wisdom with practical techniques for deciphering dream symbols.

THE 10 SECRETS TO BECOMING RICH ACCORDING TO THE BIBLE

Based on the valuable Proverbs of King Solomon, this book will guide you through ten key teachings that will help you live in abundance and make your money prosper in the modern world.

Over the centuries, King Solomon has been revered as one of the wisest and richest monarchs in history. His divine wisdom has stood the test of time, offering timeless advice on how to achieve financial success, live in abundance, and wisely manage resources. This book explores the ten secrets revealed through the Holy Scriptures, presenting principles of practical wisdom that can guide you in managing your finances.

King Solomon teaches us that money, if used wisely and with a righteous heart, can become a powerful tool for doing good, building, blessing others, and fulfilling the projects God has placed in our hearts. Solomon's life and teachings are a beacon illuminating our path, reminding us that true wealth does not lie in material possession but in the ability to live according to divine principles of generosity and justice

Prepare to immerse yourself in timeless lessons and

discover how the ancient wisdom of King Solomon can transform your life. This book is not just a read but a call to action for those who wish to improve their economic and spiritual lives. Each chapter is designed to help you reflect and put Solomon's principles into practice in your daily life.

This book will guide you through ten fundamental secrets that can help you better manage your resources and live a full, abundant, and happy life in accordance with the divine plan. Get ready to see your life transformed in surprising and wonderful ways as you embrace the eternal wisdom of King Solomon. Open your heart and mind, and allow these ancient truths to guide you toward a life full of prosperity, peace, and blessings.

Devotional Notebook
(version for men or women)

The Christian Devotional Journal is a work designed specifically to guide Christians in the journey of spiritual growth, intimacy, and connection with God. This journal offers a dedicated daily space for prayer, meditation, and listening to the voice of God, allowing men to find inspiration and reflection in faith.

Special Features:

Daily Devotional: Each page offers a complete daily devotional with space for Bible verses, teachings, reflection prompts, and prayers. Everything you need for your time of intimacy with God.

Space for Notes: Take notes, write your prayers, reflections, and thoughts as you immerse yourself in the word of God.

Listening to God: This journal offers a space for

notes that encourages you to develop a deeper relationship with God.

Elegant Design: With a sturdy cover and elegant design, this journal will be a devoted companion and beautiful to carry anywhere. It can also be a great gift for your friends in Church.

WRITE YOUR BOOK!

As an evangelical apostle, I understand the importance of spreading the word of God through various forms of communication.

Writing a book offers you the opportunity to expand your ministry and share your experience and wisdom with a wider audience.

If you have a story, a teaching, or a message to convey, I am here to support you in the writing process.

LDN EDITIONS provides consultation, support, and can take care of all aspects of your book, promoting and distributing it in different countries around the world and in various languages.

Do not hesitate to contact us. We aim to publish books by authors with important, prophetic, and consecrated messages that can transform nations.

 www.ldnonline.org
www.facebook.com/mapLDN

Printed in Dunstable, United Kingdom